SCHMUCKS!

SCHMUCKS!

Our Favorite Fakes, Frauds, Lowlifes, Liars, the Armed and Dangerous, and Good Guys Gone Bad

JACKIE MASON

AND

RAOUL LIONEL FELDER

Collins

An Imprint of HarperCollinsPublishers

HarperCollins books may be purchased for educational, business, or sales promotional use. For information please write: Special Markets Department, Harper-Collins Publishers, 10 East 53rd Street, New York, NY 10022.

First Collins paperback edition published 2007

The Library of Congress has catalogued the hardcover edition as follows:

Mason, Jackie.
 Schmucks! : our favorite fakes, frauds, lowlifes, liars, the armed and dangerous, and good guys gone bad / Jackie Mason and Raoul Lionel Felder. — 1st ed.
 p. cm.
 ISBN 978-0-06-112612-3
 1. Celebrities—Humor. I. Felder, Raoul Lionel, 1934– II. Title.

PN6231.C25M37 2007
814'.54—dc22

2006051921

Designed by Fearn Cutler de Vicq

ISBN 978-0-06-112613-0 (pbk.)

08 09 10 11 12 WBC/RRD 10 9 8 7 6 5 4 3 2 1

We dedicate this book to the men and women
of our Armed Forces, both past and present, who have
made and continue to make it possible for us to be able
to name anyone we see fit a schmuck.

CONTENTS

INTRODUCTION
Who Are You Calling a
SCHMUCK?

Back at Irving's delicatessen, at the daily morning board of directors meeting of the retired, the retired from being retired, and the she'll-drive-me-crazy-if-I-don't-get-out-of-the-house group, the insults dart around the table like hummingbirds with hemorrhoids.

The targets range from the current disposition of the world, its leaders, its catastrophes; commentaries on the relative competence (and mostly incompetence) of local doctors; the list of who in the neighborhood has died since yesterday's meeting; the comparative crappiness of recent movies, television shows, loud music, restaurant food in general (and Irving's in particular); lost financial opportunities (let's just say that we were all on the way to buy Microsoft at two dollars a share but we stopped to tie our shoes and if it weren't for that shoelace, we would be worth $400 million today); landlords (they should all drop dead by Thursday); the weather; diets and digestive problems, and on and on.

As one might expect, in situations where topics of such great pith and import are discussed, the language suits the event, animated almost to the point of geriatric violence. ("If he had said *one more word,* I would have . . .") Needless to say, the words *schmuck, putz, schnook, schlemiel,* and *schmendrik* resonate as clearly as a battleship's Klaxon sounding general quarters.

While all these words fall under the general rubric of "jerk," a person skilled in the subtle nuances of their meanings uses them with the precision of a brain surgeon dissecting a ganglia. Or at least with the skill of Irving cutting pastrami, allowing just enough fat in each sandwich so as not to cause a blip on the radar screen of the customer's taste buds thereby engendering a loud cry across the delicatessen: "Irving you *gonif*. I'm paying for pastrami, not fat." It is with this great degree of care and consideration that we use the word "schmuck" to describe and characterize the chosen people in this book.

"Schmuck" is not just a word; it is a word with DNA. It has been filtered through thousands of years of a people's suffering. It survived the steaming shtetls, insinuated itself into the patois of every city, slum, ghetto, and village in America. It has grabbed footholds in television, print, radio, and every sleazy and elegant nightclub stage, and has made its way into the mutterings of wives, mothers-in-law, business partners, tenants, teenagers. Until it found its final place of permanence (and internment, some would say) among the palm trees and condominiums of Miami Beach.

Throw the word schmuck at a person, and it is an irretrievable dagger flung. It doesn't kill, but it wounds—condemning the victim to the hell of trivialization. Mike Tyson, at one particularly low point in a career full of them, said that he felt like "a schmuck." Even Tyson, that great philologist, parsed the word properly and did not call himself a "putz." (A quick Yiddish lesson: Though schmuck and putz have the same literal meaning—penis—putz is far higher on the Richter scale of insults. Put another way anatomically, the difference between being called a schmuck and a putz is the difference between being described as an ass and an asshole.)

And so we have included under this cozy category all manner

of fakes, frauds, idiots, lowlifes, and good guys gone bad. We have searched the world—and indeed, in some cases, history itself—for our list of schmucks. Happily, and with the greatest respect, we have concluded that anyone can be one.

Even you.

HOLY
SCHMUCKS

TOM CRUISE
In serious need of a couch . . .

We're not in the habit of making fun of the mentally ill, but is there any other way to explain what happened to one of the biggest and best-loved movie stars in the world?

Looking back, we probably should have seen it coming way back when he stripped down to his underwear, picked up a microphone, and then lip-synched on that couch. Anyone who could wriggle like that on a sofa without the slightest hint of shame was someone to be watched. And, possibly, medicated.

Granted, that first couch episode was for a movie role. But when you think about it, so was his recent trampoline session on *Oprah*. (And, really, didn't his mother teach him to keep his feet off somebody's couch?) This time around, Cruise was playing the part of a middle-aged man in love. His soon-to-be child bride—a girl who during the week of their engagement posed for the cover of *Teen People*—admitted that when she was younger she had a poster of Tom Cruise up in her bedroom. Personally, we believe it's a good rule to never date a girl who's younger than your oldest shirt.

Not that Cruise chases only the young; just the clueless. How is it that so many women can keep their eyes wide shut to this wackjob? It's not exactly a secret that he belongs to a cult—sorry, religion—called

Scientology. These people actually believe that the earth was created by aliens (and they don't mean folks from Mexico).

As for their religion's founder, what's his basis for divinity? Was he born on Mount Olympus? Did wise men bring gifts when he was born? Did he see a burning bush? No, he wrote science fiction books.

We're all for religious tolerance—you want to worship Captain Kirk and Mr. Spock? Live long and prosper. But how much tolerance has Tom Cruise been showing lately?

He told poor Brooke Shields that she shouldn't be depressed after having a baby. And how does Top Schmuck know this fact? Did he go to medical school and not tell anyone? Did he even go to college? No, he knows this because, as he told Matt Lauer, he has studied "the history of psychiatry."

Ohhhhhh . . . well, why didn't you *say* so? That changes everything, Dr. Freud! In that case, we have the first patient for you. He's waiting right over here.

In the mirror.

HUMORLESS MUSLIMS

Ever wonder why there's no such thing as jiha-ha-had?

In 2005, *Jyllands-Posten,* a Danish newspaper, published several cartoons that made fun of the prophet Muhammad. And incidentally, the cartoonists were not condemning Islam; they were satirizing terrorism. Were they offensive? Maybe. Blasphemous? To some. And what was the response from the fundamentalist Muslim world?

We watched the television coverage of a Muslim religious leader screaming in an unintelligible language. On the bottom of the screen a translation appeared in English, stating that whoever drew the cartoon should have his hands cut off. So much for a slap on the wrist.

Could you picture a Jew, a Catholic, or even a Latter-Day Saint calling for the death of a cartoonist? Come to think of it, could you imagine a Jew killing anybody for such meaningless reasons? If a Jew becomes angry, he might sneak into your house and snatch your Lipitor. Or if he were more cunning he would make a deal with your doctor to lie about your cholesterol number. Or on Yom Kippur, he might steal the matzo ball soup, pot roast, and kugel from your kitchen counter for the break fast.

We never met Jewish men involved in pointless struggles. That is why you seldom see Jewish football players. A Jew is not going to risk spraining a neck or tearing a knee ligament to battle somebody about catching a ball. A smart Jew would rather go to a sporting goods store and buy another football to avoid the conflict. This is also the reason why we never see Jewish hockey players. Hockey players spend the entire game hitting each other in the mouth with sticks. When Jews saw how gentiles played hockey, it was an incentive to become dentists.

In addition, Jews do not have the reputation as street brawlers or fighters. People are unafraid of being clobbered by a Jew. Did you ever hear anybody say, "Don't go into that Jewish neighborhood! There are a lot of accountants over there!" Did you ever hear of four black people walking down the street say, "Lookout, there's a Jew over there!"? Jews have been accustomed to threats and persecution for thousands of years and would never foster needless violence because Jews have always been grateful for places to live in peace.

But radical Muslims have decided that no boundaries, laws, or limits should impede their homicidal behavior. Their beliefs are twofold: the right to take a life and also the right to rob everyone else of freedom of expression.

Meanwhile, the world reacted with an amazing cowardice to these Muslim attacks against Denmark and other Western countries where the cartoons were displayed. Instead of expressing a collective fury, the world pleaded for forgiveness and promised not to offend with any more cartoons. Could any acts be more cowardly and perverted?

These same Muslims who are not offended by suicide bombers, terrorists, and repeated destruction worldwide viewed the cartoons and exclaimed, "*Oy vey,* this is so terrible!"

Each day, Muslim and European newspapers slur and degrade Jews as animals and rodents. Did you once hear of any Jewish authority cry out for the heads of the cartoonists or that they should suffer some murderous end? There is no record of any Israeli hit squad pursuing cartoonists. If Jews applied the same sadistic standard about injurious cartoons as the Muslim world, no Muslim would be safe in any country.

Besides, no one ever died from a cartoon. If the worst act the Nazis ever committed was to draw those offensive stereotypical caricatures instead of operating the death camps, six million Jews would be alive today.

When was the last time any country decided to execute a Muslim because of some affront? Yet, the Muslim world has created a new international statute called "The Insult Law." This means that they believe they have the right to kill anyone whenever it pleases them. And there is nothing you or any nation can do to prevent it.

If a Muslim walked down a street in Israel with an insulting cartoon in his hand, no Israeli would threaten the man's life. The Jew would be joyous that it was a cartoon and not a bomb.

Obviously, we don't see harm in satirizing other religions. But humorless fundamentalist Muslims (is that redundant?) feed on controversies such as this one, exploit a situation resulting in an angry mob shooting rifles in the air, embassies being torched, and non-Muslims being massacred in the streets—preferably in front of the international press so the whole world will watch. (At least in the United States, on those rare occasions when people do riot, they have been smart enough to concentrate on stealing television sets and packages of frozen chicken wings.)

Meanwhile, no one is safe from these hair-trigger jihads. Not even the pope. In September 2006, Pope Benedict XVI cited an obscure 14th-century text that mentioned Muslims in a speech. "Show me just what Muhammad brought that was new, and there you will find things only evil and inhuman, such as his command to spread by the sword the faith he preached," the pope said, quoting a Byzantine emperor.

He might as well have drawn a cartoon. Immediately, Muslim leaders called for "a war against the worshipers of the cross." (Though we're sure they'd also be happy to throw in some Star of David worshipers just for fun.) So what did the pope do? Did he use the opportunity to speak out against this hateful hypocrisy?

No. He apologized. And quickly.

And for what? Because he interpreted certain basic Muslim teachings as encouraging violence in the name of God and, as a man of peace, spoke out against such activities? His interpretation is *his* interpretation and he certainly owes no one an apology—especially since he read the words as they were clearly written. Having got past the irrefutable logic of the foregoing, one must ask, how many times have the Muslims apologized for the pain and suffering that their terrorist organizations have committed? While we hate the terrorists, we constantly reaffirm our respect for their religion and the people of their faith. We believe common decency dictates that we should protect blameless Muslims from the crimes of the guilty. It's ironic that while we are protective of innocent Muslims, despite so many acts of terrorism, the imams of the world could announce a sentence of death upon any people because of perceived or imaginary insults.

How did the Muslims decide that they have the exclusive right to freedom of speech? How did they achieve the right to say and do whatever they please, while the rest of the world has the right only to listen, cower, suffer, and sweat? While the leaders of the non-Arab world plead with their populations to protect Muslims from any act of discrimination, the Arabic leaders, both religious and political, encourage vengeance and violence against people of other religions. Logically speaking, if a mere insult deserves a sentence of death, acts that cause the destruction of human life deserve the same fate.

Countless times Muslims have insulted people of every faith. The fact is, in their mosques and public speeches and in every kind of media, their insults and abuse of other faiths is limitless. If you visit any Arab city, on the pages of every newspaper and the walls of virtually every building you'll see articles, pictures, and paintings insulting, degrading, and dehumanizing people of every other faith. While they practice acts of humiliation against every other faith, isn't it strange that no leader of any other religion has ever considered any act of retribution or even discrimination against the Muslims? Has anybody ever refused to marry a girl because she has a Muslim brother? Has anyone ever refused to kiss a girl because she has a Muslim father? Or left a table in a restaurant because he had an Arab waiter? Nobody has ever refused a toasted bagel because it was made by a Muslim baker. Or refused to buy a Slurpee in a 7-Eleven because of an Arab storekeeper.

How long will it take for humanity to put an end to this kind of helplessness and cowardice in the face of this inhumane behavior? Instead of cowering in fear of losing our lives from the hands of fundamentalist Muslims, we should immediately and firmly advise them that any act of violence against innocent people will be met with a level of aggressive response that will make them realize that acts of terror against innocent people will cause them to pay an unbearable price.

We'll make them watch an episode of *South Park*.

JEWS FOR JESUS
And now, a reading from Jackie 3:16 . . .

First of all, let's consider the very name of this organization: Jews for Jesus. Are there not enough Christians in the world? Did somebody misplace a billion Chinese?

And what exactly, you may ask, is Jews for Jesus anyway? Would it surprise you to learn that the group was founded in San Francisco in the 1970s? Of course not. Where else could it have started but the hippy dippy capital of the world? It turns out a man named Moishe Rosen (so far so good) converted to Christianity when he was 17 and became a Baptist minister. Somewhere along the way Reverend Moishe decided that he wanted to convince Jews that Jesus was the true messiah but that they could still be Jewish.

Forgive us, but we've heard this one before. Like in ancient Rome—right before they decided that Jews' hands would look better with some nails in them. Or in 15th-century Spain, when a few old Jews were put on a table and asked—not so politely—if they believed in Jesus. And in Weimar Germany, which was also very accepting of Jews who wanted to believe in Jesus.

But even wanting Jews to believe in Jesus isn't our real problem with these *meshuggehs*. Our beef is that they had the nerve to distribute some promotional literature using Jackie's name and likeness in a way that implied he was a member of their organization.

"Jackie Mason . . . A Jew for Jesus!?" the brochure read. Please. Jackie has been and will always be a Jew. (This will no doubt come as a disappointment to some self-hating Jews who wish Jackie weren't one.) He responded to this disgusting abuse of his name by stating, "While I have the utmost respect for people who practice the Christian faith, the fact is, as everyone knows, I am as Jewish as a matzo ball or kosher salami." He's an ordained rabbi, for chrissake. (Granted, he stepped down after a few years to become a comedian, but, hey, someone in the family had to make a living.)

And just to prove once and for all that Jackie is Jewish, we did the one thing any self-respecting Jew would do in this situation.

We sued the bastards. It took a federal lawsuit to make them apologize and cease distributing the offensive pamphlets.

MADONNA
Funny, you don't look Jewish.

Over the years we've known a lot of Jewish girls who like to pretend they're shiksas. They'd dye their hair blond, wear headbands and pearls, name their daughters after jewelry stores. These women were never going to fool anyone, but if cutting off your nose to spite your religion makes you happy, who are we to argue?

And then there's Madonna.

We know, we know, she studies kabbalah more than a yeshiva full of rabbis. But those red bracelets she wears make her no more a Jew than wearing a yellow bracelet makes you Lance Armstrong. She's even taken to calling herself Esther. She's as much an Esther as she is a Madonna. (Say what you will about the real Madonna, but at least she was a virgin.)

And what's with the phony English accent? Madonna grew up in Michigan, so why does she speak like Maggie Smith? Also, she was born a Ciccone. Now, apparently, she's trying to convince us that back in the old country her people were known as Ci-cohen. Frankly, we liked her a lot more when she was dancing around in fishnets and that cone bra, shtupping Warren Beatty.

And now because the world stopped paying attention to her for 20 minutes, Madonna has started buying—okay, *adopting*—African children. She has already introduced her Malawian son, David, to kabbalah. Trust us, this kid was happy just being introduced to food. Okay, Madonna, we get it, you've gone from material girl to maternal girl. Mazel tov.

Now if you really want to be a Jewish mother, expect your ungrateful kids not to call.

REFORM JEWS
Funny, you don't sound Jewish.

Consider the classic story of that nice Jewish boy from Minsk named Sean Ferguson. When asked how he acquired this Irish name in 1911, Ferguson replied, "I was born Schlomo Krapotnik and came from a long family of rabbis. During the voyage to America, I was ill with a high fever and suffered horrible seasickness. When the man at Ellis Island asked my name, I was loopy with fever and could only reply quietly in Yiddish, *Schön vergessen* ("Woe is me, I forgot my name!"). That's how I became Sean Ferguson."

At Ellis Island, immigration officers, besieged daily by the befuddled masses arriving from Eastern Europe, had neither the time nor the patience to write down the exact names of these new arrivals. Thus, another kind of circumcision was performed, and a family from Poland disembarked steerage class as the Buckowitzkis and strolled onto Manhattan as the Buckmans.

Reform Jews, meanwhile, love to boast how proud they are to be Jewish but they're getting their noses done and changing their names every day to appear more gentile.

The final step in the assimilation of these third- and fourth-generation Reform Jews has produced some attention-grabbing first-and-last-name combinations like Tiffany Schwartz, Reginald Rex Isaacson, and Ashley Lipshitz. But one couple moved farthest to that perfect state of Jew as gentile naming their son Crucifix Finkelstein. (Oddly enough, black people in America are the only ones who retain Jewish names—like Whoopi Goldberg.)

These Reform Jews will also invent crafty stories to describe their facial features, none of which they designate as Jewish. Praise a Jewish girl who's had either a good or bad nose job by telling her that she looks beautiful for a Jewish woman, and she won't hesitate to stab you in the heart. Darker-skinned Jews from the tanning salons will boast how people mistake them for Greeks, Italians, or other Mediterranean peoples. Ralph Lauren meet Sophia Loren.

To pass for a gentile, Jewish men look like they dressed in a closet without a light, putting on brown shoes, white socks, green pants, and topped by a tam o'shanter. For stylish Jewish women, the only designers to consider are French. No yenta is going to march down Fifth Avenue in the Easter Parade and brag, "Look, I'm wearing a Horowitz." In fact, the newest style for Jewish women is to wear designer labels *outside* their clothes. We even know a clothing manufacturer in Manhattan's Garment District who has become rich by selling authentic labels from Christian Dior.

One famous Reform Jewish congregation on Long Island is so assimilated that the rabbi is a gentile. This is the same synagogue that is always closed on the Jewish holidays.

To all these Reform Jews, we say *dayenu!*

Not that they know what that means.

AL SHARPTON
Praise the lard!

We actually kind of admire Al Sharpton, the longest, unsustained, unsponsored carnival in America. For 20 years, he has managed to jump from one major scam to another. (And at his size, any kind of exertion is pretty impressive.) Instead of preaching to the masses, Reverend Al prefers swimming in mirages, and inhabits an upside-down world of false statements and innuendo. It's a world that we don't quite see clearly but, we have to admit, thousands of his followers do.

Sharpton brings to his unsavory history a hoax more daring and dangerous than one any sideshow barker could concoct: the Tawana Brawley episode.

To review: In 1987, a 15-year-old black girl named Tawana Brawley claimed that six white men had raped her and covered her in feces while shouting racial slurs. Without waiting for an official police investigation, several well-known black activists hurried to Duchess County, New York, and hitched their wagons to Brawley's star as her advisers, including Sharpton and two world-class race-baiters named Alton Maddox and C. Vernon Mason.

The trio accused a local white prosecutor, Steve Pagones, of being one of the rapists. The only problem was, Pagones didn't do it. For that matter, nobody did. Brawley made the whole thing up. And Sharpton and his pals were all too happy to help her. (Pagones eventually sued and, 11 years later, won a libel verdict with Sharpton owing $65,000, which was paid by the late Johnnie Cochran and others.)

Sharpton is always going for the gold and, oddly, he found the answer to financial improvement in the discovery of an unusual weight-loss program. Call it the Vieques Diet.

In 2001, a group of politicians, activists, and celebrities headed to Puerto Rico to be arrested on purpose for protesting the naval bombing on the island of Vieques. The New York politicians who were arrested in Puerto Rico received free airline tickets back to New York; however, Sharpton did not. He needed two seats on the aisle and also half of the opposite aisle.

Unfortunately for Sharpton, a federal judge in Puerto Rico decided to make a federal case out of the protest, literally, and sentenced big Al to 90 days. The other three defendants received 40-day sentences, but because Sharpton had made other illegal protests over the years the judge added an extra 50 to his incarceration.

Sharpton was held in the Metropolitan Detention Center in Brooklyn, and upon arriving at the jail he announced that he would stage a hunger strike. When he was released, it was reported that he had lost 15 pounds—which is roughly the equivalent of tearing a page out of the New York phone book. (We'd give the man a hand for his efforts, but we're afraid he'd eat it.)

And what will this heir to P. T. Barnum do for his next act?

When it was rumored he was hondling to appear in a television show called *Al in the Family,* Sharpton admitted that he had greater ambitions: he was considering a run for the White House (whose very name he probably considers racist) in 2008. Perhaps he could be the first president impeached *before* he was elected.

And one more thing—who thought it was a good idea to make Jesse Jackson the arbiter of racial healing? That makes as much sense as Ted Kennedy being a lifeguard at a girls' school.

RICH

SCHMUCKS

DAVID H. BROOKS
How much is that bar mitzvah in the window?

At our bar mitzvahs many years ago, we read the Torah in an architecturally challenged and run-down local synagogue. The ceremony represented the serious occasion at age 13 when a Jewish male was recognized as an adult in the religious community.

We dressed in our first-ever long-pants suit (traditionally, the color was called "Brooklyn bar mitzvah blue") and we wore a tie clip, a relic of male attire as forgotten today as spats.

Attending the event were our family, a few close friends, along with some drowsy old Jewish men who had come to attend an armistice celebration in 1918 and remained asleep in the pews ever since.

If the bar mitzvah occurred in winter, a few neighborhood people, Jewish and non-Jewish, came to doze in a room that was warm. A guy always showed up called Schlomo Kornheiser whose avocation was crashing every bar mitzvah in the borough for a free meal.

Then at the end of the bar mitzvah, after the "today I am a man" speech (or, if you prefer, "today I am a fountain pen"), we all went around the corner to an inexpensive cafeteria for some barley soup, a sugar cruller, and a glass of tea.

There, the entertainment consisted of Aunt Molly and Uncle Saul tapping out "My Yiddishe Momma" with teaspoons on the glasses along with a few people stamping their feet out of rhythm. Everyone had a good time and that was that.

But today, American bar mitzvahs are no longer the simple and elegant ceremonies that move nice Jewish boys to manhood. These lavish events have become more elaborately planned productions than most Broadway musicals. Everyone makes a bundle—caterers, musicians, florists, and photographers. And of course a new profession has been created: event coordinator, a kind of Martha Stewart for bar mitzvahs. Only Jewish.

(By the way, it was in 1922 when 12-year-old Judith Kaplan, the daughter of a progressive rabbi in New York, strode to the *bimah* and read a portion of the Torah in a book form. This was the first recorded instance of a bat mitzvah, where a young Jewish *girl* came of age. From that moment on, Conservative and Reform families began lavishing the same amount of ostentatious cash on a daughter as a son.)

We thought that some limits of propriety existed for the new superdeluxe coming-of-age events for the progeny of emperors until we learned of the bat mitzvah thrown by defense contractor David H. Brooks for his daughter Elizabeth in New York's Rainbow Room.

Now, pick a number that would seem shocking to spend on a 12-year-old's party. Go on, pick one. What would make you nauseous: $50,000? $100,000? $1 million?

Try $10 million. That's right, $10 million. For $10 million here's what else can be purchased: the services of the New York Mets' relief pitcher David Wright for an entire season including spring training and any possible postseason play; 30 Rolls-Royces; a comfortable apartment overlooking Central Park; 20,000 hookers of the highest quality.

But here's what David Brooks got for his money: he hired Steven Tyler and Joe Perry of Aerosmith, 50 Cent (who is apparently mispriced), and other musicians to perform in front of his daughter and her friends.

Brooks is the CEO of DHB Industries, a Long Island–based

company that makes body armor and, because of the war in Iraq, also makes a bundle. This fact alone should have cautioned against a vulgar public and outrageous expenditure of money.

And it's because of this schmuck that some little girl in the future will whine, "Daddy, I thought you loved me but you only spent $9 million on my bat mitzvah."

THE HILTON GIRLS
You can't spell hotel without "ho."

These girls never had a chance. A moron daddy, a gold-digging mommy, and a fortune to burn on designer doggie clothes pretty much sent the Hiltons down the path of questionable taste straight from their mother's gilded womb.

And yet, must they impose their vulgarity on us every single day? There are plenty of spoiled, little rich girls in the world, getting drunk and vomiting on their fancy high-heeled shoes and we never have to see videos of their train wreck lives—let alone their sexual antics. We don't have to hear about their shipping heir boyfriends or their eating disorders or their inability to stand upright after midnight. In proper wealthy families, shame is still a dirty word, and trashy harlots who malign the family name quickly get sent to boarding schools or rehab. Or they get the ultimate revenge and marry a short, bald, Jewish billionaire.

Not so with the Hiltons, whose own mother has been known to flash her penthouse in public now and then. (And speaking of *Penthouse,* how long before this family becomes the first to pose together in their altogether?) Instead, Paris and her less offensive but still irritating sister, Nicky, are paid to go to parties, where they are photographed in varying states of chemically and genetically induced idiocy—and undress—the results of which are plastered on our daily newspapers next to actual headlines about war, famine, and real estate.

The Hilton girls are basically famous for being famous, which, while pathetic, would not be so terrible if they had even an ounce of charm. Or talent. Yet they persist, tabloid cockroaches, unstoppable and unavoidable, infesting our media with their insolence and their singularity of purpose: to be seen, even if it means being obscene.

To which we say, do us all a favor, and get a room.

HOWARD SCHULTZ
His cups runneth over . . . and they runneth over us.

L et's start with what we like about Howard Schultz, the CEO of Starbucks: He was born in Brooklyn.

Here's what we don't like: If we said to you, "Here's a great idea for business. We'll open a new kind of coffee shop. Instead of 60 cents a cup, let's charge $2.50, $3.50, $4.50, and $5.50. For each additional French word, add another $4.00. Also, there will be only a few tables and chairs, no busboy, and the customers will clean up after themselves *and* tip the help."

Would you say, "This is the greatest idea for business ever? We'll put two on every corner!" No, you would place us in adjoining cells inside an insane asylum.

Need a refill in a regular coffee shop? They give you a fresh cup for free until you drop dead from a caffeine overdose. You can come in when you're 27 years old and keep drinking coffee until you're wearing Depends (which if you keep drinking all that coffee, you'll be needing sooner than you think).

A refill at Starbucks is $1.50. Two more refills will run you another $4.50. For four cups of coffee, you could end up paying $35.00 and taking out a second mortgage.

To our tastes, the coffee at Starbucks tastes a tad on the burnt side. If we get burnt coffee in a regular coffee shop, we call a policeman and say, "Officer, this coffee is the dregs from the bottom of the pot." But when it tastes burnt at Starbucks, people exclaim gleefully, "Ooh, it's a special blend from a rare bean from the highlands of eastern Cabomba in Central America! Also . . . I asked for soy milk."

Many Starbucks do not provide enough chairs and customers have to sit on high stools. You probably haven't been on a stool this high since you were two. Now 93-year-old Jews are hiring Sherpas to reach the top of these highchairs. Finally, upon reaching the top, they can't drink coffee because 12 other people are also crammed around the one tiny table.

Do we exaggerate? Do you know that if you buy a bagel at Starbucks, you pay extra for the cream cheese? It costs an additional 60 cents. To use a plastic knife on the bagel is another $32. If the knife touches the bagel, it's $48. That bagel with a thick schmear will eventually cost you around $312.

The person at the cash register has a large glass that says "Tips." You're carrying your own coffee and waiting to sit for an hour—now you owe the serving staff extra money?

Also, you see a sign that says, "Please clean up when you're finished because there is no waiter or busboy"? Now you've switched jobs from waiter to janitor. A group of elderly Jews can tidy up a Starbucks in an hour and a half.

And Starbucks can get away with this only because they have fancy French and Italian names for everything. Will there be a city, town, or hamlet in Europe or Asia that will escape the ubiquitous sameness of Starbucks? And how long before the first Starbucks opens inside an existing Starbucks?

On second thought, why didn't Howard Schultz ask us to be investors?

LARRY SILVERSTEIN
Freedom Towering Schmuck.

Before the rubble had been removed from the World Trade Center, Larry Silverstein, the owner of the property, embarked on two shameless campaigns: brazen attempts to, one, recoup double the fair and reasonable payout of his billions of dollars in insurance claims and, two, to introduce his oily personage to New Yorkers as the put-upon victim and grieving landlord.

Silverstein, backed by a number of investors, had signed a 99-year lease for the World Trade Center a mere *seven weeks before the attacks*. He was awarded an insurance payment of more than $3.5 billion to settle the claim but the voracious landlord sued the insurers for an additonal $3.5 billion, claiming the attacks represented *two* separate events. Right, just like God handed down five commandments—twice. Or, if a guy comes up to you and hits you with his right hand followed by his left, do you tell a cop that you were assaulted two times?

Silverstein also tried insisting on limiting the occupied height of the next tower built at the site to around 70 stories, despite opinions that the new building (or buildings) should be no shorter than the original height of the Twin Towers.

First, Silverstein exploited the grief of tens, if not hundreds, of thousands of people by taking center stage after this national tragedy. His face, which looks like he has had a fekockteh facelift done by a blind barber wearing boxing gloves, should have been reason alone to not trust him with the rebuilding of Ground Zero.

What no one expected to see on the front page in the days following 9/11 was the identity of the owner of the World Trade Towers. It should have been an obscure fact in the business section, a one-day financial afterthought to the main story of death and terror.

But the eager-to-be-photographed Silverstein was delighted to boast that he was the Towers' owner. Usually, people pretend to be used car salesmen or pedophiles rather than be identified as landlords. Not Larry Silverstein. He was so thrilled with the media attention he even utilized a public relations firm. Interestingly, in spite of what Silverstein would like everybody to believe, he put up the minority of the money for the purchase of the property.

Experts on the future development of the World Trade Center site agree that if Silverstein continues with his egotistical and unrealistic plan to build five office towers at Ground Zero, the probability is zero that these will ever be completed. New York mayor Michael Bloomberg spoke apolitically, but truthfully, when he said that Silverstein's grand plan would leave New York City "high and dry."

Silverstein's problem is that it is likely he won't find the financing to finish the job. A study undertaken by New York City predicts that Larry Come Lately will run out of money in four years.

The rebuilding of this site is a sacred commitment and we do not believe that the mercenary Silverstein has either the cash or the character to do justice to the reconstruction. Then again, what do you expect from a man who dyes his hair the color of brisket?

GEORGE SOROS
Goody Two-Schmuck.

In the movie *Being There,* Peter Sellers played the role of Chauncey Gardner, an odd character who was perceived as a genius, but might just as easily have been described as—why be politically correct?—mentally retarded.

Toward the end of the film, Gardner, a former gardener who comes to advise the president of the United States himself, is asked what he thinks of China. He pauses, bows his head, and slowly says, "China . . . is full of Chinese." The reporters listening nod in awe and murmur, "Full of Chinese. Hmm?" and then remark to each other about the brilliance of this insight.

Money also leads people to believe that those who have lots of it are as sage as Chauncey Gardner, and that each word uttered by a rich person is a cultured pearl. If you have boodles of money and speak rubbish, people will not call you crazy; at most they will label you "eccentric."

These reflections lead us to think of George Soros. He believes that his money should afford him a seat as a major player on the world's political stage. He craves to be regarded as a global dignitary whom others should listen to and respect.

Countless world leaders and captains of industry have listened with reverence to every word of this rich bastard's twaddle. The thinking of his acolytes goes something like this: "All our lives we directed our energies to making as much money as possible. But George Soros earns more moolah in one day than we earned in 20 years. Therefore, he must be a genius."

As far as we're concerned, if you pile gold on a donkey's back and send it around the world, it still comes back a donkey.

Soros flew onto our radar some time ago when he and some other bilious billionaires took out advertisements in newspapers opposing the abolition, or at least the marginal tamping down, of the federal estate tax. We, on the other hand—along with an astounding 71 percent of Americans—have always agreed with the past Republican administrations that believed the so-called "death tax" was the most unfair penalty in the panoply of the American tax system. Put simply: Why after paying all your taxes on the money you earned during your lifetime should the IRS make a killing off your dead body?

Billionaires, after all, have legions of lawyers and accountants to help them avoid paying taxes, practices that are not available to the little guy. Just how far do you figure Soros and his cronies have gone to save a few shekels in their own estate taxes? Our guess is that they have paid out more to lawyers and CPAs than most of us could possibly leave as an inheritance.

In 1997, for example, Soros and his wealthy pals in an act of extreme chutzpah founded Responsible Wealth, which is affiliated with United for a Fair Economy (UFE), a nonprofit organization devoted to putting a spotlight on the dangers of excessive inequality of income and wealth in the United States. This is the equivalent of the guy who finally buys his way into the country club and then tries to make sure that you and everyone else like you can't join.

Despite Soros's professed interest in helping people via his considerable charitable works, his past speculations in the world's currencies have wreaked serious economic havoc. Soros earned a meager $1 billion in one day in 1992 wagering that the British pound would fall, and although he has always denied it, many people believe that he was partially responsible for an Asian economic crisis in 1997 when he bet against the currency of Thailand.

If we held only those thoughts about Soros we would happily consign him to a circle of Schmuck Hell populated by other hypocrites and windbags. But we believe he is a more destructive person—a Hungarian-born Jew who escaped the Holocaust and now doesn't believe in giving money to Jewish causes.

Worse than that, the presumably self-hating Soros openly states he is no defender of Israel because "[Israel] did not express itself in a sense of tribal loyalty that would have led me to support Israel." We point out that Israel is a nation and not a tribe.

One final thought: he speaks Esperanto. Fluently.

POWER SCHMUCKS

JIMMY CARTER
It's hammering time . . .

In the famous eulogy from William Shakespeare's *Julius Caesar*, Mark Antony says, "I come to bury Caesar, not to praise him." For the Democratic Party, each death of a well-known Democrat (say, the late Senator Paul Wellstone of Minnesota) has provided an occasion neither for praising nor burying the deceased, but for using the event to pounce viciously on the Republican Party.

To us, it's a wonder that these donkeys don't stage a series of accidental deaths among some of their more famous aging personages in order to exploit funerals for the purpose of exhorting the faithful.

Recently, chief among the Democratic transgressors to have used a solemn funeral as an opportunity to deliver a political scolding to the GOP was the world's second most famous carpenter, former president Jimmy Carter. At the memorial service for Coretta Scott King, late wife of Martin Luther King Jr., Carter reminded those assembled that one way to determine that the struggle for civil rights had not ended was to "recall the faces . . . who were most devastated by Katrina—to know that there are not yet equal opportunities for all Americans. It is our responsibility to continue their crusade."

Was Carter so steeped in dotage (or did a ball-peen hammer fall on his noggin during a Habitat for Humanity barn raising?) that he failed to notice President George W. Bush and his wife, Laura, seated on the dais with the two Clintons and also, former president George Herbert Walker Bush? Why didn't Carter just come out and say, "And we Democrats intend to mark this solemn occasion of Mrs. King's death to trash George W. Bush and his administration? Now, I shall cede some time to Al Franken who will sing a few pleasing spirituals."

The liberal press consistently tells us how President Bush has misused and manipulated speaking opportunities at military bases in a phony way to take advantage of the bully pulpit and generate a positive spin on his programs in the national media. But these same lefty critics saw no harm, no foul, in the public rebuking of the president of the United States at the memorial for the wife of the great civil rights leader.

Jimmy Carter's magnanimity doesn't extend just to Americans. John Lennon once wrote, "Give peace a chance" and that's always been a great idea. But a not-so-great notion came from Nobel Prize winner Carter who suggested giving the newly elected Hamas Party in soon-to-be Palestine its chance. Too bad Carter couldn't hitch a ride on a time machine, land in Germany in 1933, and say, "Now now, let's not judge too quickly, let's give these Nazi fellas a chance."

Specifically, Carter, who was in Palestine to monitor the elections where the radical Hamas Party mopped up Arafat's corrupt Fatah Party, suggested that the United States should not stop sending funds to that country. His alternative? To funnel taxpayers' cash through the United Nations. This was akin to saying, "Hey, let's give Tony Soprano some cash to pay his parking tickets." We have seen too much of the world's money (especially the United States's) go into one side of the UN and come out the other into a secret Swiss bank account.

Carter thinks that Hamas is the dominant political party in the way the Tories control Great Britain. But the ruling Hamas members will not recognize Israel's right to exist and, in fact, are continually plotting that democratic nation's demise. Worse, in the turbulent area, with Syria and the crazed president of Iran daily preaching nuclear jihad against Israel, another well-funded enemy at Israel's border is not the best solution for a workable peace.

Thankfully, the U.S. Senate rejected Carter's Pollyannaish recommendations, voting that no aid be provided to the Hamas-controlled Palestinian Authority. If Jimmy Carter had possessed leadership skills equal to his carpentry talent, he might not have put the nails in his own coffin during his four years in the White House.

RAMSEY CLARK
If genocide is your plan, he's your man.

Usually when you ask young lawyers why they went into law, invariably, they will mention some role model like Atticus Finch or our friend, the late Johnnie Cochran. It is hard to imagine anyone this side of Adolf Eichmann being motivated to enter the legal profession on account of Ramsey Clark. In fact, every time the words "Former Attorney General Ramsey Clark" are heard on television, 4,000 existing lawyers pretend they are chiropodists.

Clark is yet another member of the Lucky Sperm Club—he had the good fortune to have a father, Tom Clark, who was a poker buddy of President Truman. This undoubtedly qualified the father to be appointed to the U.S. Supreme Court. As a member of that exalted body, Tom Clark managed to achieve the reputation of being one of the dumbest judges to sit on this bench in the last century. Ramsey, meanwhile, has proved to be a chip off the old blockhead.

In the listings in the reference guide *Lawyers in New York,* attorneys are categorized under their individual specialty known as a field of practice. Many legal specialties exist including: Criminal, Federal, State, Divorce, Admiralty, Personal Injury, Auto, Immigration, Elder Law, Real Estate, Wills and Estates, Intellectual Property, and even Traffic Violations. Under each listing are many names, but nowhere is the name Ramsey

Clark, since no subspecialty exists for the representation of Ruthless Dictators/Brutal Tyrants, his specific fields of practice.

Thus far in the world's courts, Clark has represented Yugoslavian mass murderer Slobodan Milosevic, ex–Nazi concentration camp honcho Karl Linnas, and Elizaphan Ntakirutimana, an architect of the African genocide in Rwanda. Alas, Hermann Göring's suicide cost him another potential client.

Clark has never met a cruel tormenter he didn't look forward to representing. He was an integral part of Saddam Hussein's defense team in the homicidal dictator's screaming show trial in Iraq, and he stormed out of the courtroom when the Iraqi judges had the temerity to ask that he address the court in a language they would understand.

Perhaps he would understand the word schmuck.

BILL CLINTON
Liar, liar, underpants on fire.

The politicians who rule our lives can be heroes or scoundrels. The problem for the American electorate is that it never knows whether it's voting in a gem or a rhinestone, a winner or a loser, an Abraham Lincoln or a Warren G. Harding. At each election, we hope the next new mayor, governor, senator, and, most of all, president, will fulfill our expectations—and maybe, if we are lucky, even a campaign promise or two.

The reality is that politics is more important to us than morality. If some political lowlife lies to advance a cause we believe in, we stay silent. No one in the United States cares for the truth if that truth damages the policies of his party.

And so, we have been witness to the nation-deflating scandals of JFK's Bay of Pigs, Richard Nixon's Watergate, and Ronald Reagan's Iran-Contra, but no politician has lied so consistently and pathologically as President Bill Clinton. The Maharajah of Mendacity. A prevaricating weasel of the lowest form. Of course, he didn't lie all the time—only when he talked.

Whether it was offering up nights in the Lincoln Bedroom to big donors, last-minute pardons for pay, or the White House silver— everything in the Clinton administration seemed like it was for sale.

Even his home state of Arkansas suspended his law license because he committed perjury in the Paula Jones case. In other words, he was too big a liar even to be a lawyer.

But the ladies sure loved him. Gennifer Flowers. Paula Jones. Monica Lewinsky. And those are just the names we know about. Everybody always asks: If Bill Clinton was so busy chasing girls, how did he manage to take care of the country's business? How? It takes five minutes to commit adultery—maybe ten if you accidentally picture Helen Thomas—and he still had the rest of the day to be president. (Ironically, while in the Oral Office, Clinton had his *dog* neutered. So perhaps the dog acted like the president while the president could act like a dog?)

Frankly, we also lost respect for the Secret Service during the Clinton era. The Secret Service is supposed to protect the president from every possible harm—yet it failed to step in front of a schlumpy yenta in a beret.

In the end, though, people who rationalized Bill Clinton's extracurricular behavior had to use Sigmund's Freud's analysis when characterizing the president. A gentleman, Freud asserted, was a man who didn't have an erection with *every* woman he met.

Then again, it's a big country.

HILLARY CLINTON
Blowing harder than Monica Lewinsky.

Forget for the moment about all of the lying, the cheating, the records that were discovered only *after* the statute of limitations ran out, the investments that netted 100 percent profit in a short period of time, the renting of the White House beds, and the pathological covering up for her husband. We have the uncharitable thought that if Hillary Clinton has an eye on the presidency, how can anyone believe she is going to acquire and act on knowledge concerning the intentions of foreign countries (like Iran) when she could not figure out that her husband was shtupping every woman under the age of 80 in her *own* home?

What ticks us off most about Hillary these days is her foray into bigotry and her attempt to fan the flames of prejudice and class hatred. In a speech to an African-American church in 2005, she stated that the Republican majority in the House of Representatives "operates like a plantation." As if that wasn't awful enough, she said this on Martin Luther King Day. And just to drive the point home further, she added, in a lower tone and in a most conspiratorial manner, "*You* know what I mean."

Hillary Clinton was willing to exploit part of this nation's shameful past for her own political ends. If Mrs. Clinton was serious about her effort to capture the African-American vote, the way to win their hearts was not to make remarks about slave plantations. Mostly everyone believed the statement was ridiculous and offensive. But why should that surprise us? After all, this was the same woman who also once claimed to have Jewish roots.

Recently discovered DNA proved that all Eastern European Jews descended from four Jewish women who apparently carried a gene for having headaches whenever sex was involved, and a predilection for the wearing of small animals as coats. A few years before she decided, "Maybe I'm also a Jew," Mrs. Clinton willingly embraced Mrs. Yasser Arafat, who enjoyed voicing the calumny that Israelis used poison gas on Palestinian children. Even with our fertile imaginations, we cannot understand, if the Palestinians were living among the Jews, how the gas went up the noses of only Palestinian children? Was the suggestion that the Jews knocked on the doors of each Palestinian, asked if children were inside, and, if yes, handed the inhabitants gas? Even the international community, which is pro-Palestine, did not take this dumb and false charge seriously.

When she ran in the 2000 New York State senatorial race, the Republican Party put up a token candidate, Rick Lazio. He was tossed into the ring (headfirst) after New York City's Mayor Rudy Giuliani withdrew from the contest. Giuliani was ahead of Clinton in the polls, but had to drop out when he discovered he had prostate cancer. In the debate, when Lazio tried to hand Mrs. Clinton a piece of paper that contained a pledge he had signed, and asked her to sign it too, suddenly we heard an uproar from liberals claiming that he had "violated her space." Left-wing commentators likened the paper attack to the Rape of the Sabine Women.

Any concern about the principle of "violation of space" did not seem to prevent her from basically *selling* space in the White House. Rich Democrat contributors who normally vacationed in the south of France contacted their travel agents for package deals to enjoy paid-for time shares in the Lincoln Bedroom. Inside, posted on the closet door, was a sign that read, "Best Offers Accepted to Avoid an Early Check-Out Time." The Clintons basically ran a hotel for wealthy donors.

If the late John Gotti was known as the Teflon Don, then Hillary Clinton should be the Teflon Prima Donna, given her history of having skated, skirted, evaded, or conned her way out of every possible criminal culpability.

A British company sold Dubai Ports World the management rights of some ports in the United States. The Democrats and also many Republicans reacted negatively to the deal, claiming the nation's security would be breached by an Arab-controlled company managing the ports and maybe even a new terror attack would arrive by next Thursday.

What few people understand is that foreign ownership in America is very common, including radio and television stations. Additionally, half a dozen federal agencies vetted the sale and uncovered no security or fiscal problem. Dubai had been the country's ally in the war against terrorism since 9/11. Finally, the U.S. Coast Guard, Customs Service, and the Treasury Department have the responsibility for overseeing port safety and security.

Stephen Flynn, a security expert with the Council on Foreign Relations, pointed out that Dubai Ports World "basically operates the cranes, loads cargo, and shuttles containers around the yard" while Americans do the heavy lifting, and usually these longshoremen are not the kind of people that Arabs would want to bump into on the piers.

Overnight, the Ports Affair heated up to superfluous scandal and at the forefront stood Hillary Clinton with her megaphone. She became one of the main critics of the Bush administration's deal, ascribing evil motives to the Arabs' desire to manage our ports. As she was pointing the finger, her husband was receiving $600,000 in speaking fees from Dubai and also received a $1 million gift for the Clinton Library (the only presidential library, presumably, with an X-rated section). It seems that

Slick Willy arranged for his former press secretary, Joe Lockhart, to be the public relations point person for Dubai on this ports deal.

The old saw that the right hand doesn't know what the left hand is doing and vice versa paralleled the Clintons's statements on Dubai, another indication that there is clearly no pillow talk in this marriage. We are certain that if Bill Clinton were still in the White House, there would have been a logical reason for the lack of spousal communication. The White House contains so many rooms it was possible for the Clintons to spend weeks inside without ever seeing or talking to each other.

However, in Chappaqua, New York, where they currently live, they share a smaller home and meeting by chance in the kitchen cannot be avoided. So, how could Bill not know Hillary's position on the Dubai project? If she assumed as many positions with her husband in the bedroom as she has in Washington, this would be a happy marriage.

RANDALL "DUKE" CUNNINGHAM

The best congressman money could buy.

W hen it comes to spotting a lowlife, a crook, a phony, or double-talker, always ask a poor person. The downtrodden have a graduate degree in being shafted, conned, lied to, and generally ripped off so they know how to pick 'em.

But there seems to be a serious disconnect between brains and common sense among polite middle-class folk unaccustomed to wholesale robbery, especially from a trusted eight-term U.S. congressman and former U.S. Navy Top Gun pilot. Even though Randall "Duke" Cunningham drove around in a Rolls-Royce, owned a 42-foot luxury yacht and lived in a $2.5 million home, once again the average person thought, "This enormous wealth is simply an indication of what a genius guy he is."

Cunningham must have been the smartest person in government this side of Hillary Clinton. She invested $10,000 and a week later made $100,000—which is a better return on an investment than even the Mafia can offer.

In 2005, the outspoken and acerbic Republican Cunningham, representing the 50th Congressional District in California, went public with a tearful mea culpa and pleaded guilty to conspiracy to commit bribery, mail fraud, and wire fraud. However, months before, he had stated, "I haven't done anything wrong."

These crimes and ethic violations were spotted only *after* 2003 San Diego newspaper reports questioned a defense contractor's purchase and subsequent sale of Cunningham's home. The contractor accepted a staggering $700,000 loss on the home and this lowball sale happened eight months into the booming real estate market.

Something smelled gefilte fishy.

The U.S. Department of Justice thought so also and began an investigation of Cunningham, who sat on the House Defense Appropriations Subcommittee. Oh, and that defense contractor who was such a poor real estate speculator? Turns out he had received tens of millions of dollars in contracts.

Since 1991, Cunningham has been depicted as a colorful congressman and his Vietnam War "ace" image made him an appealing member of the House of Representatives. He was an expert on security and naval warfare and was considered tough on crime (apparently other people's crimes and not his own). He also had quite the reputation for mouthing spiteful remarks and, at one time, said that the Democratic Party leaders in the House should be "lined up and shot"—which is a rather extreme way of dealing with criticism—although it does have the attractiveness of permanency. Also, it's cost-effective.

Sometime in 2000, Cunningham either conceived of a plan to sell his access or was approached by outsiders with an offer he couldn't refuse. Astonishingly, no other person in Congress (not even the opposition) questioned his newly found wealth. By the time investigators closed in, he had accepted $2.4 million in bribes.

Cunningham pleaded guilty and said, "I learned in Vietnam that the true measure of a man is how he responds to adversity." It was also revealed that this Judas wired himself up to help the Feds catch others.

The ignominious end came when he was sentenced to eight years for bribery. His final words prior to sentencing were "No man has ever been more sorry."

Or maybe he was just sorry to have been caught.

AL GORE
Inconvenienced by the truth.

We like a man who lies for a good reason. For instance, on her wedding day you should always tell a bride she looks gorgeous, even when she resembles a prune Danish that's been left overnight on the sidewalk. Meanwhile, you should always tell *your* wife, who has a face like *yesterday's* prune Danish, that you were up all night with a sick friend. Likewise, you tell your boss, who is so dumb he received a refund from a mind reader, that he is a combination of Albert Einstein and Noël Coward.

You recognize that each one of these is a lie, but at their worst they are born out of sensitivity or kindness. But in each instance, these lies are told for a specific reason. When Bill Clinton, that all-world liar, fibbed, it was always for the same reason: he was either trying to defraud, cover up, or con the public.

Not so with Al Gore.

Gore had already established his bona fides on environmental issues (for better and for worse) and had even been anointed "Mr. Ozone." So why, when he was campaigning a few years ago, did he tell students in Concord, New Hampshire, "I found a place in upstate New York called Love Canal. It was I who had the first hearings on the issue. I was the one who started it all"? The Love Canal he was thinking about probably had to do with a motel outside of Buffalo, since this environmental nightmare that everyone associates with that name was a moribund issue by the time of the committee hearings. In fact, Love Canal had already been declared a disaster area when Gore discovered the problem, and everyone there had moved away.

And while we're on the subject of love canals, Gore's defense of Bill Clinton throughout the Monica Lewinsky scandal was simply unconscionable. Sure, you should always defend your boss in public. Even if he's a schmuck. Even if he's the most powerful schmuck in the world. But let's state once again for the record what Bill Clinton did while president of the United States: He had adulterous sex with a younger woman employed by the White House *in* the White House and, later, was found guilty of perjury and obstruction of justice for which Congress voted to impeach him—and for which he lost his license to practice law in Arkansas.

So how did Al Gore, that great moralist, view Clinton's extramarital nookie in the most sacred building in the United States? "I think that whatever mistakes he made in his personal life," Gore said, "are in the minds of most Americans balanced against what he has done as president." Boy, you could fuel a lot of hybrid cars with fertilizer like that.

As for his own presidential aspirations, we thought Gore had taken his hanging chads and gone back to Tennessee after the 2000 election. And for a while it seemed as if he had done the noble thing, retired permanently into the background to do good works and lend a name to worthwhile domestic and international projects and maybe do some part-time fibbing. Oh, and make a lot of money. He may not have invented the Internet, but with the amount of Google stock Gore owns, he might consider buying it.

Then we saw his movie *An Inconvenient Truth* and guess who looks like he's ready to run again? You want to know why there's global warming? It's because Al Gore goes around the world gassing on about it.

THE NEW YORK TIMES
Unfit to print.

In most instances in life it is impossible to be both giver and receiver. When a baseball is thrown, there is a pitcher and there is a catcher. In a holdup, one person is clearly holding the gun and the other obviously has his hands in the air. But in recent years, the *New York Times* has managed to be both the perpetrator and victim at the same time, a victim who blamed the perpetrator who, it turned out, was the same person as the victim.

We present the confusing saga of the disgraced *Times* reporter Jayson Blair.

When this journalistic fiasco first occurred in 2003, and Blair was accused of plagiarizing *and* fabricating stories—capital crimes in the newspaper world—newsstand sales of the *Times* did not suffer nor did it lose any advertising. In fact, it was able to cut out the middleman, since it not only made the news, but it also reported on it. In a brilliant move, it gave itself an exclusive without its own reporters ever having to leave their desks or to make outside telephone calls.

Meanwhile, when they weren't gloating, the rest of the media were relegated to reporting the story when the so-called paper of record *was* the story. Talk about phony reporting: the *Times* created its own spin so that others in the media could only do secondhand reporting.

Was this fit news that only the *Times* could print?

So how could this happen to the venerated *New York Times?* It all goes back to an affirmative action policy taken to absurd extremes, when the paper hired and then coddled Blair, a young black reporter who was out of his league. Blair was plenty smart, so smart that he figured a way to generate exclusives in his underwear. He never had to leave his apartment or to interview anyone, and thus avoided the problem of ever printing, "No comment."

The paper's irresponsible pursuit of affirmative action sheltered Blair in a cloak of journalistic inattention that no other *Times* reporter—black, white, pink, or polka dot—enjoyed. Once having hired Blair because he was black, the editorial board decided that it could not treat him as it did the other reporters or hold him to similar journalistic standards. The situation was analogous to the one that found Mayor Bloomberg being accused of forcing the NYPD to meet ticket quotas, a charge he angrily denied. (He stated that the police did not have quotas; they merely had to meet "performance goals.")

Howell Raines, the executive editor of the *Times* during the Blair affair, later admitted that in hiring and firing the black reporter he had acted "like a white man from Alabama." Luckily for Jayson Blair, Raines acted this way in 2002—life could have been very different for him in 1862. The point is that in hiring Blair, regardless of whether Raines "acted like a white man from Alabama" or an albino from Tulsa, it should not have influenced his responsibility as the editor of the world's leading newspaper.

It should be noted that the American Society of Newspaper Editors has suggested that by the year 2025, 38 percent of all newspaper employees should be members of a minority. Maybe it should be 90 percent or maybe 10 percent. Or maybe the Tulsa albino should be hired because the supply of albinos from Oklahoma is limited? Or perhaps, perish this unworthy thought, people should be hired and fired because of their performance and ability.

It was the mismanagement by the *Times* of its standard policies that was directly responsible for the reporter's actions. Yet, the newspaper shrewdly played the victim. The media reported how Blair had misled and deceived the *Times* (victim). And after his resignation, the victimized *Times* acted promptly to attack the perpetrator (*Times*). It was as though the *Times* picked itself out of a police lineup as the mugger who attacked it.

After Blair made a hasty retreat, the *Times* conducted a town hall meeting, a sort of journalistic perp walk. Arthur Sulzberger Jr., the paper's publisher, informed the paper's staff that he would not accept Raines's resignation if it was offered. Then, true to the tradition of accurate reporting, surprise, Raines did resign, and to no one's astonishment, Sulzburger accepted it.

To tell you the truth, as long as he was in the mood, we wouldn't mind if Sulzberger accepted a few more resignations—namely those of Frank Rich and Maureen Dowd. Or is it Maureen Rich and Frank Dowd?— we sometimes have trouble telling these two knee-jerk liberal columnists apart. (By the way, how do you think they decide which one of them gets to be the left knee?)

Frank Rich is a very smart and ethical guy, but how he got to be an op-ed columnist in the first place is beyond us. He started out as a theater critic, after all. Apparently if you can write some mean reviews about Andrew Lloyd Webber—and Rich was known back in those days as the Butcher of Broadway—you're qualified to comment on world affairs. (And for the record, Rich has actually said some nice things about Jackie over the years, although he did once mention that Jackie was his "second most dreaded act on *The Ed Sullivan Show*"—after Topo Gigio.)

Now, instead of criticizing Hamlets, he gets to throw eggs at the president. His latest book, *The Greatest Story Ever Sold,* is all about how President Bush's administration has lied to us since 9/11. Talk about the Gray Lady calling the kettle black.

Dowd, meanwhile, also likes to make jokes about President Bush and his cabinet, often using cutesy names, like referring to the president as "Bubble Boy" and calling the former secretary of defense "Rummy." Her last book, *Are Men Necessary?*, asked lots of empty questions about women's careers and marriage.

We have a question of our own: Is Maureen Dowd necessary? Discuss.

Meanwhile, one last thought occurs to us: If men are not necessary, then there would be no women, which would leave us with a race of cockroaches, none of whom would carry enough money in their pockets to purchase the *New York Times*.

KEITH OLBERMANN
The O'Schmuck Factor.

Keith Olbermann is a cable TV loudmouth who thinks he is the liberal answer to Bill O'Reilly. About the only thing he has in common with O'Reilly is that their last names begin with O.

Olbermann first became famous as one of the smart-aleck anchors on ESPN's *SportsCenter.* Maybe his shtick was funny when he was delivering baseball scores, but now he's delivering the news. As far as we're concerned, leave the jokes to professionals.

Each night on *Countdown with Keith Olbermann*—or as it's known to some, *Putdown with Keith Olbermann*—he names the "worst person in the world," a distinction that often goes to his nemesis, O'Reilly. Honestly, with all the legitimate lowlifes in the world, he thinks Bill O'Reilly is even close to the bottom? (We'd recommend that he take a look at our table of contents, but God forbid he should name a fellow liberal.)

Naturally, President Bush and members of his cabinet are frequent targets of his facile rants. But he's even been known to take shots at his fellow MSNBC hosts, once claiming that "Rita Cosby is nice but dumber than a suitcase of rocks." That's class.

If all Olbermann did was pontificate each night like a sophomoric Edward R. Murrow (he's even had the chutzpah to use Murrow's famous sign-off, "Good night and good luck"), we might be able to ignore him. And given that Olbermann's network is MSNBC, that's basically what people do. But last summer he did something so hateful that it can't go unmentioned.

While making an appearance on the Television Critics Association press tour, Olbermann walked onstage holding a Bill O'Reilly mask and proceeded to give the audience a Nazi *Sieg Heil* salute.

After being chastised later for making this despicable gesture, the cowardly Olbermann told Jay Leno that he was just saying "yoo-hoo" to a friend. Sure, and when Hitler did this he was just waving back to Heinrich Himmler. Olbermann then added that Bill O'Reilly has "defended the Nazis" on various occasions.

Is Keith Olbermann the worst person in the world? No. Just an enormous schmuck.

NANCY PELOSI
Shrieker of the House.

So the Democrats finally won something. Mazel tov. Now what? They're going to fix Iraq overnight? Rebuild New Orleans? Find Osama Bin Laden? So far, all it looks like they're interested in doing is registering for new White House china patterns for Hillary Clinton in 2008.

But along with the new Democratic majorities in the House of Representatives and Senate comes a first in United States history: a woman will be Speaker of the House.

That the woman who's now wearing the pantsuit has long been one of President Bush's biggest detractors, concerns us tremendously. After all, she once called the president "incompetent" and that kind of petty name-calling has no place in serious American politics.

What's even more disturbing is that Pelosi came into office claiming that the "Democrats pledge to make this the most honest, ethical, and open Congress in history." It was a boast that was downright Clintonian in its hypocrisy. Within days, she nominated Representative John Murtha, an unindicted co-conspirator in the infamous Abscam bribery case of the 1980s—for a leadership post. The Democrats wisely didn't elevate Murtha, but the ensuing controversy caused Pelosi to withdraw her support for another tainted Democrat she wanted to appoint to a key

House committee—Alcee Hastings. Before he was a congressman from Florida, Hastings was a federal judge charged with bribery and perjury. He was acquitted at the time, but in 1988 was impeached for the same charges by the House. (Nancy Pelosi, it must be noted, voted for that impeachment.)

If that's the kind of ethical governing the Botox-addicted Pelosi and the Democrats plan on doing for the next two years, they might want to hold off on measuring those White House drapes.

GLOBO-SCHMUCKS

AFGHANISTAN
War stinks. Or at least smells.

In between keeping an eye out for terrorists, paying our brothers-in-law to open any suspicious mail we receive (which is the only work these guys have done for pay in years), and following President Bush's advice to spend as much money as possible, we have not had time to solve the problem of Afghanistan. But we do have some helpful suggestions.

We knew Trenton, New Jersey, was located somewhere between New York City and Miami Beach, but, because it was reputed to be a place that harbored terrorists, we looked further into its location. It turns out terrorism was only about 50 miles southwest of Manhattan.

So, no one could make fun of us for being nervous, since the president stated after 9/11 that he would attack not only terrorists but also the skunks who harbored them. Okay, that explained the smell across the river. We used to look up at the Manhattan skyline to see whether pigeons were dropping any greetings, but now we would have to make sure that nothing more dangerous was coming our way from Trenton.

We cannot blame the Afghans for being confused. First, we bombed their country and afterward we dropped food. This doesn't make sense. First we should have dropped food. *Then*, when they came out for food, we should have dropped the bombs. But to eradicate the Taliban using food generally seemed a pretty inefficient method of killing them.

(Unless of course we dropped food prepared by our mothers-in-law; then the Taliban would have surrendered, begged for mercy, and pleaded for Maalox. Trust us, a little overcooked brisket and we would have had Osama within a week.)

One fact has continually puzzled us about the past bombing; in most wars, houses are bombed so that bad guys are forced to hide in caves. But in Afghanistan, the terrorists began by living in caves. Through our constant bombing, we not only created new caves for them, but in doing so, we also enlarged the living space of their existing caves. How did Martha Stewart miss this opportunity for a whole new line of furniture?

Those who did surrender, however, posed a new kind of problem for our troops: stench warfare. Since no running water flowed anywhere near the Taliban caves, the men our troops captured had a distinct odor problem. So when the Afghanis surrendered in large numbers, at first our troops demanded that the enemy put their hands up, but after a few unsavory whiffs, our military never accepted surrender without putting on gas masks.

The situation in Afghanistan, and later in Iraq, also apparently created a global shortage of those burqa-wearing virgins. (And speaking of burqas, who could fall in love with a tablecloth?). Turns out, Bin Laden promised each of his followers they would be rewarded with 40 dewy-eyed lovelies in heaven. But at the rate the Taliban were being exterminated by Allied bombing or otherwise dispatched and sent on ahead to greet Allah, the supply of virgins dwindled. To tell the truth though, we also had that same virgin-shortage problem back in the old neighborhood. You get over it.

MAHMOUD AHMADINEJAD
The Ayatollah of crapola.

In 2005, there was another highly public hostage-taking event in Iran, and this time it was not a group of Americans; it was historical truth. The newly elected president of that Muslim country, Mahmoud Ahmadinejad, the former mayor of Tehran, and a former ringleader in the 1979 Iranian kidnapping, stated publicly that the Nazi Holocaust of World War II was an invented European myth.

So, what else is new in the Middle East? There, Holocaust denial is as much a commodity and staple of hatemongering against the Jews as eating a hummus burger at the corner falafel stand. To many, most noticeably this Iranian president and the revolutionary Hezbollah Party in Palestine, anti-Semitic statements are a lot tastier.

Ahmadinejad achieved the double goals of inflaming worldwide public opinion by his false and hateful remarks, and also of sending a direct message to his nation's fundamentalists that he would continue the late Ayatollah Khomeini's revolutionary promise "to wipe Israel off the map."

We can understand why the average Iranian might initially be swayed by Ahmadinejad's empty rhetoric, since we believe three facts in life are permanent: death, taxes, and anti-Semitism. But this sleight of hand will fool people only once. If he can't put food on the tables of Iran, those same people won't care what horrors he mouths about Israel or the Holocaust, or the 40 virgins waiting for them in heaven.

A point arises when even a lowlife Iranian content to blame Jews for all the misfortune in life will lust for at least one virgin before he makes the trip to the big mosque in the sky and perhaps even a pastrami sandwich with Russian dressing and coleslaw.

FRANCE
Fifty million Frenchmen *can* be wrong.

Are the French a nation of lowlifes? Has glory faded from this once major player on the world's stage? Do they continue to be, in the words of the great philosopher Bart Simpson, "cheese-eating surrender monkeys"?

In a word: *oui*.

How else can you explain why our NATO ally—one that consistently proclaims itself to be America's good friend—resists our best efforts to bring democracy to the Middle East?

To be fair, France was once a courageous nation with brave warriors. Indeed, there might not have been a United States had the Marquis de Lafayette not fought alongside George Washington at the Battle of Yorktown. And say what you want about Napoleon, but he was no sissy. (If anything, the poor bastard didn't have the sense to know when he was beaten.)

General Charles de Gaulle? He's credited with realizing that after the trench warfare stalemate of World War I, advanced developments in tank design and a new combat strategy would define the future of combat. In typical French military tradition, however, his papers were ignored by his own army and studied by the Germans, who turned de Gaulle's strategy into the blitzkrieg. *Au revoir*, Paris. *Wilkommen*, Vichy.

After World War II, de Gaulle served as France's premier, and said about unifying his nation, "One can't impose unity out of the blue on a country that has 265 different kinds of cheese." In other words, *merde* happens.

Another prime reason for treating the French as scum is their horrendous treatment of food as art. The overblown term for this first-class dining is *haute cuisine,* which translates to "high cooking," a term no phony American gourmand would dare say. It is always the fancy French term that is used.

Our first gripe about the high cooking is the teeny-weeny portions. The meals in French restaurants are served in the smallest amount that legally can be called a main course. Often, you need a magnifying glass to see the food. The piece of steak (for which you're paying top euros) is often found by peering under the string bean. If you ask the waiter, "Where's the beef?" he will have to lift up the diced carrots, or move the string bean aside to reveal it. The French also like to call their food *nouvelle cuisine,* which, freely translated, means no food on an enormous plate.

The tiny amount of food is the prime reason for the low lighting in French bistros. By the time you've adjusted to the darkness, the waiter has slapped the check on the table.

The next complaint is that French dinners are more the creation of an artist than the chef. The food looks beautiful, sculpted and arranged in an eye-appealing way with layers of colors and odd vegetables carved to resemble the Eiffel Tower or Rodin's statue *The Kiss.* We don't know whether to eat some dishes, offer them up for sale on eBay, or freeze it until the *Antiques Road Show* comes to town.

But the ultimate French cuisine rip-off is escargots. These, as anyone knows, are snails. Snails are slimy and vile looking, the vermin of the shelled world. You wouldn't capture and cook a snail unless starvation loomed around the corner. But when in France, Americans delight in ordering this vile creature because they love pronouncing the name in round French vowels: "ESS-CAR-GOH."

If escargots were so delicious, every coffee shop in America would have them on the menu. However, they would not be served in the French style heaped with garlic in the shells but rather Americanized and ordered at diners as "Snails and Swiss cheese on toast," or "Two eggs sunny side over, home fries, and snails."

Also, in New York, you go into a coffee shop and someone gives you a friendly but insincere hello and hands you a piece of cake. In a Paris café, the waiter ignores you for an hour and then brings you a tiny cup of espresso with one lump of sugar. You can always get more sugar, of course—if you have another hour to kill.

And let's not even talk about the smell in France. On second thought, let's. Somewhere along the way, the French decided that it was better to take the country's water and bottle it rather than to use it for the weekly bath (the genesis of the invention of perfume and cologne). The excess of unused water allowed French companies to market the bottled version to American phonies who would pay big bucks to drink this *water* at fancy, overpriced restaurants.

About the nicest things we can say about France now is that they gave us Impressionism, the Statue of Liberty, and the freestanding street *pissoire* where you can take a private leak in public.

GEORGE GALLOWAY
A not-so-great Scot.

Americans have a sickness: We believe that anybody who speaks with a British accent must be a genius—or at least, somehow related to Winston Churchill.

When we read about Scottish lout George Galloway, a current member of the British Parliament—and an outspoken hatemonger against America, Israel, and even his native Great Britain—we flashed back on the image of a man who learned from infancy that the only way to gain attention was by purposely soiling his diapers and throwing temper tantrums in public.

Galloway is a prime example of a facile wordsmith, a master debater who has fallen in love with his faux bullyboy persona and his odious politics. For more than 20 years, his most notable success has been to keep his dapper mug in front of the public—first in Britain and now the world—by making outrageously negative and destructive comments. (His second wife, a Palestinian Muslim, publicly accused him of being unfaithful during their marriage.)

After the murderous attack on British citizens in July 2005's suicide bomb attacks in the London Underground, Galloway offered a perfectly clear rationale for why the carnage had occurred: "We argued, as did the security forces, that the attacks on Afghanistan and Iraq would increase the threat of terrorist attacks in Britain. Tragically, Londoners have now paid the price of the government ignoring such warnings."

The egregious statement of innocent Londoners "paying the price" represented yet again his callously indifferent remarks about Arab-sponsored terrorism. He was a vocal foe of both the Gulf War in 1991 and the 2003 invasion of Iraq. He said, "Fallujah is Guernica. Fallujah is a Stalingrad"—conveniently ignoring the fact that in both of these cases Fascist forces were attempting to overthrow a lawfully elected government)—"and Iraq is in flames as a result of the actions of these criminals [George Bush and Tony Blair]."

Apparently, he feels more sympathetic to the murderous Taliban and their favorite terrorist guest, Osama Bin Laden, than to the victims of the British-born Muslim bombers. Galloway's finger-pointing always starts with the USA or the UK and never points to the terror cells of the Middle East. He even appeared on Al Jazeera television to criticize Blair and Bush in a move reminiscent of Hanoi Jane Fonda.

For all the many admirable causes that Galloway has advocated over the years, his main focus seems to be keeping the name George Galloway in the limelight. Also, on occasion, this sham working-class anti-hero has lived the high life of champagne and caviar, and often, dashing off into the sack with unnamed women.

Galloway has spent a lot of his time justifying scandalous remarks, defending hints of fiscal impropriety, and using libel litigation against the media. He is sharp-tongued, clever, and not afraid to go toe-to-toe with the British Parliament. Yet, despite all these antiestablishment shenanigans, thankfully, he has never attracted a wide audience in his native country, nor has he ever merited the political respect due a worthy intellectual opponent who espouses obvious contrarian views.

Not that it's always worked. Galloway was kicked out of Britain's Labor Party in 2003 after making contentious statements that brought the party to disrepute "through behavior that is prejudicial or grossly detrimental to the Party." The decision to expel him came after he was interviewed on Arabic Abu Dhabi TV, which is managed by the United

Arab Emirates' largest media group. He proclaimed that, for the military situation in Iraq, "the best thing British troops can do is refuse to obey legal orders." This comment brought him close to being tried for treason under Britain's 1934 Incitement to Disaffection Act.

Galloway will forever be linked to Iraq through 15 years of visits and meetings with Saddam Hussein and the dictator's deputy prime minister, Tariq Aziz, the smooth-talking Groucho Marx look-alike, now awaiting trial, who was once the eight of spades in the U.S. military's playing card deck of the most-wanted members of Saddam Hussein's government. He is perhaps best remembered for being interviewed on television in Baghdad, proclaiming that the Americans had been defeated and that the city remained untouched. Unfortunately, the camera panned behind Aziz showing the military and government building being blown to bits as he spoke.

Galloway always stood against the United Nation's Iraq sanctions, having preferred to let Saddam remain in power to continue the genocide of Kurds and the murder of dissidents.

In 1998, Galloway founded the Mariam Appeal, an organization with the charitable intent of bringing to light the suffering of sick Iraqi children as a result of UN sanctions against that nation. Money was raised for this good cause but negative allegations of extravagant spending surfaced. Galloway has denied charges that Mariam laundered oil-for-food profits or that he was ever involved in the trading of oil vouchers.

What's not in dispute is that he took money from the government of Pakistan for the weekly *Asian Voice,* which produced favorable coverage of the Benazir Bhutto regime. Nor is it in question that he regards Fidel Castro's Cuba as a "model for the world," or that he also once described the Cuban leader as "the greatest man I have ever met." Or that he has expressed great admiration for the Soviet Union, saying, "I think the disappearance of the Soviet Union is the biggest catastrophe in my life."

So, we ask, simply, if George Galloway has so many friends in these low places, why doesn't he emigrate to Havana, or Moscow, or perhaps a nice vacant cave in Afghanistan?

THE INTERNATIONAL
RED CROSS
When you bitch upon a star . . .

Not even the most virulent anti-Semite with a broken leg would say to a Jewish physician, "Don't fix my leg, you Jew bastard."

The Indonesian authorities, however, did not have even that much common sense. After the devastating tsunami in 2004, Israeli Red Cross workers, world-class disaster specialists, were denied entrance to provide needed medical and emergency aid to a small, seacoast village that was predominately Muslim.

The reasoning of the Indonesian brass went something like this: Initially, the villagers would have cheered as the relief truck headed their way but, when the vehicle drew near, they would turn away in aversion because the wagon displayed a six-pointed Jewish star. The poor natives would prefer to drown, be miserably sick, and remain injured rather than accept assistance from Jews.

The life-saving team of medical workers would have come from Magen David Adom (MDA), the Israeli equivalent of the Red Cross. The MDA has been in operation for more than 75 years and has brought emergency help to people of all races and ethnicities.

What occurred in Indonesia has historical roots in the brainless position of the International Red Cross in Geneva since it does not officially recognize the red Star of David as part of its global organization, consisting of 192 countries.

The reason offered for this continuing ban against the Israeli organization is that, IRC officials argue, the Star of David represents the flag of Israel and it would signify a specific country and not an ambulance. Sure, if you saw a white vehicle painted with a red Star of David, with an ear-splitting siren blaring, racing toward some tragedy, would you think that it's speeding to an accident to render assistance or making an emergency bagel delivery?

The two symbols that are officially recognized by the International Red Cross are a red cross and a red crescent. White vehicles with these symbols indicate emergency worldwide aid and they are guaranteed free access by the Geneva Convention, even in war zones.

We understand why the International Red Cross would reject certain other religious symbols as being unsuitable for markings on ambulances. A few that come to mind are the Serpent Wheel, the Pentagram of Satan, and the Big Hanging Salami from Katz's Delicatessen.

Likewise, other nonreligious red symbols would be inappropriate for placement on international emergency vehicles. These include red herrings, red lobsters, red-hot chili peppers—and of course a Red Hook, which is a section of Brooklyn so rough that today even the Red Cross would have to pay protection money before sending in an ambulance.

Recently an ingenious solution was offered to redress the ban against Israelis' MDA and, more important, to devise a universally acceptable symbol that could be used on all ambulances to signify emergency aid. The suggestion is to use a red diamond on the theory that inside that diamond another symbol could be used: a red cross, a red crescent, or even a red six-pointed star.

The Swiss are behind this proposed compromise and their intelligent reasoning is that countries with multireligious populations can either place multiple symbols within the red crystal or leave out all the symbols. We realize that the outer diamond shape opens a possible Pandora's box, by allowing for the placement of any religious symbol inside. But honestly, in a disaster situation we could not care less who brings us emergency medical services—even if the ambulance is painted with a portrait of Hillary Clinton . . . well, maybe not Hillary Clinton. We have to draw the line somewhere!

SAUDI ARABIA
Barrels of Fun.

O ther than the togas worn in the days of the Holy Roman Empire (which was hardly holy or Roman, and which, eventually, no longer even qualified as an empire) we never cared much for men who wear bedsheets as clothing.

Like the Ku Klux Klan.

And the Saudis.

American presidents, but particularly Bill Clinton, could not have treated the Saudi monarchs any better if they expected to find that their sheets covered the curves of an 18-year-old belly dancer. But it was not daydreams of suntanned flesh that tilted American policy toward the Saudis. Rather, it was our national thirst—President Bush called it "our addiction"—for the black gold known as oil.

The Saudis control 25 percent of the world's oil reserves and this has allowed them to blackmail us. For decades, successive American presidents have acted as if Saudi oil was more important than Israeli blood. Now, finally, President Bush seeks to curtail our dependence on oil through new initiatives involving other fuels. Any move is a plus that promotes independence from relying on Arab oil. Especially when you consider who has the second-largest reserve of oil: Iran.

Consider this lesson from American history: As the United

States expanded westward, settlers were initially divided between farming and raising cattle. Water was often scarce and situations often arose when water was unavailable downstream and a payment was made to an upstream neighbor to procure some. If the money demanded was reasonable, then compensation was made and everyone benefited. However, if the tribute demanded was too great, or impossible to pay, the settlers resorted to force, so that the water flowed freely.

If oil is so vital to our way of life (much as water was to the early American settlers), then there is no good reason why we cannot simply take over the Saudi and Iranian oil fields with a force of arms, pay a fair price for the oil, and distribute it on an equitable basis to the world. We could establish a democratic government around the specific wells—much in the way we looked after the Panama Canal. This would ensure the flow of oil for decades and the world would benefit from this trickle-down effect by the establishment of reasonable prices. And this would force at least a portion of these Arab countries to be democratized.

The common refrain that America should not be in the nation-building business is nonsense. In the past, we were successful in rebuilding Japan and Germany, both of which were converted from despotic terror states to thriving democracies.

There is a tendency to make orgies of inaction in the name of geopolitics and the endless pleasures of contemplating and recontemplating actions and possible reactions. Here the course is simple, and the rewards immediate and direct.

By now it should be abundantly clear—even to the Arabists in the State Department—that the Saudis are no friends of the United States. It was not by some geographic happenstance that most of the terrorists who attacked us on 9/11 came from Saudi Arabia. Let's never forget that Osama Bin Laden is also a Saudi citizen, and it should be mentioned that he paid terrorist gangsters, also mainly Saudis, who now enjoy our hospitality in the guarded cells of Guantanamo Bay.

The Saudi people celebrated when the World Trade Center and the Pentagon were attacked. They still continue to fund terrorist training schools to produce another, larger generation of youthful suicide bombers. Saudi foreign minister Prince Saud al-Faisal made clear the country's position when he refused to permit American military bases on Saudi soil in the war against Iraq.

The respected Washington think tank the Rand Corporation offered this opinion to the Pentagon: "The Saudis are active at every level of the terror chain, from planners to financiers, from cadre to foot soldier, from ideologist to cheerleader . . . Saudi Arabia supports our enemies and attacks our allies."

Certainly, responsible leaders of our government see Saudi Arabia for what it is, a repressive, autocratic state unfriendly and hostile to America. Indeed, Saudi Arabia is antagonistic to the principles of Western civilization, adhering instead to a culture more devoted to the Koran's teachings, such as: "Then, when the sacred months have passed, slay the idolaters wherever you find them."

Unless they're talking about O. J. Simpson, no thank you.

BENON SEVAN
Putting the UN in unctuous.

Benon Sevan is unknown to almost everyone except Kofi Annan, the former secretary general of the United Nations. The secretary probably wishes he had never heard of this native of Cyprus, who allegedly had his hand in the UN cookie jar. And let's face it, anytime you hear the word "allegedly," you can bet it's true.

Sevan was the executive director in charge of the controversial $64 billion Oil for Food Program, a UN-sanctioned project (under the aegis of the Security Council) that offered humanitarian aid to the Iraqi people during the period when the UN mounted sanctions against Saddam Hussein's regime.

But after an independent assessment of the program by Paul Volcker, former Federal Reserve chairman, Sevan was accused of taking kickbacks totaling more than $150,000 over the four-year period he was in charge of the UN program.

This amount was chicken feed, of course—assuming there are still chickens to feed in Iraq—compared with the billions that Saddam siphoned off from the program for his own use.

When first confronted with these charges, Sevan left for Australia and moved into a kangaroo pouch to think it over. After a month, he returned to New York, where he resigned his office.

If bribery can be proved, then Mr. Sevan certainly should be in the *Guinness Book of World Records*. He achieved the outstanding trifecta, because he was able to screw the people of Iraq, the folks at the UN, and the well-intentioned citizens of America all at the same time.

If Sevan is convicted, he better think about going back to developing a meaningful relationship with that kangaroo, since his love life in jail will be considerably less pleasant.

DR. HWANG WOO SUK
Send in the clones.

The shocking news coming out of Asia made us want to drown in a bowl of tepid borscht. For if you cannot trust a South Korean scientist, whom can you trust? We speak of Dr. Hwang Woo Suk, who claimed to have developed a method for human cloning. Dr. Roh Sung, his colleague, basically said that Suk's results sucked and were fabricated.

Hwang rushed to the hospital to be treated for stress—which is another way of saying he was caught with his genes down.

So, we had to postpone plans to give each other clone jobs as this year's Christmas (oops, we can't say that anymore)—*holiday* gifts.

Over the years, we grew weary of the repetitious sessions of two-handed card games, playing cribbage or gin. Time and time again, if we could clone ourselves, we could play four-handed games of bridge, hearts, or even whist. To be honest, we were fed up talking to each other, and looked forward to what the other's other might say.

We would reduce the possibility of a hernia lifting heavy objects, when eight hands could handle the task more easily than four. If we decided to become gentiles and play squash, we would not have to work up a sweat, allowing our clones to do the running and the shvitzing.

What about being accosted by irate husbands? We could say, "No, crazed spouse, it wasn't me; it only looked like me. In fact, it's him."

Pointing to the clone head. "Go right ahead. Bust that philanderer a good one in the nose."

As for those two redheads we made a pass at and who shot us a nasty look as though we were leftover *kasha varnishkas,* let our clones take the sharp rejection. But if the redheads warmed up, at the crucial moment the clones could step into the next room and allow the A-team to take over.

We conceived of many other opportunities for sending in the clones: fittings at tailors, buying the evening paper in snowstorms, being able to make whoopee with a stewardess and her roommate at the same time, proctology exams, Sunday family dinners, and taking our places on jury duty.

Call us selfish and lethargic, but we envisioned that as we worked on coprojects, we could always send out the clones for coffee and cake.

Our scientific cloning unhappiness began with Dolly, the first ever animal to be cloned and our favorite sheep. This undoubtedly must have been an event of much joy in the Arab world, well known for the romantic relationships the men have with their flocks. Frankly, we never felt an attraction to these wooly creatures, although you can save money by not having to buy them dinner and a movie, or ending the evening in a wrestling match in the back seat of a car. The sheep would not have the nerve to ask for a mink coat.

Dolly died prematurely in 2002 after living for six years and having several offspring. After Dolly's unfortunate premature demise, we were double-punched by Dr. Hwang's distressing confession about the falsification of his cloning data.

In both of these cloning incidents, we spotted a problem with animal or human cloning for the future. Maybe the idea that we could go to bed early while our clones took our girlfriends out for dinner and dancing and returned them after we were fast asleep was not an idea whose time had come.

We consulted our pal Manny, the resident medical expert, who lost his pharmaceutical license by confusing the bottles of Viagra and Monoxidil, thereby causing the guys in the neighborhood to have to walk around with stiff hair standing up straight. He explained to us, at our daily meeting at Abe's Delicatessen, that what people do not realize is that, although an animal clone will be a physically exact copy with the same DNA, its personality will be different. Pet owners who broadcast that they'll be happy to shell out $50,000 for a carbon copy of their beloved Fluffy are bargaining for serious kitty trouble. That formerly mildmannered feline may now be poised for the kill, claws extended and ready to leap at Grandma's goiter, mistaking it for a fat rodent—arguably the same mistake that Grandpa made.

We're the first to admit that although clone Raoul II would look identical once the beard had grown in, it is doubtful that he would have the command of the law or suffer the attendant heartburn. As for cloned Jackie II, he may turn out to have the humor of a defrocked Presbyterian rabbi.

Alas, it seemed that Dr. Hwang faked all of his results. Benny's wife, Tiffany, in what turned out to be a neighborhood scandal, told everybody after the divorce that she also had been "faking it" for years. Benny then made the same confession. Afterward, Tiffany's boyfriend and Benny's girlfriend also admitted the faking, and so it went on and on until it seemed everybody in the neighborhood was a fake. But nobody was hurt by these bedroom revelations.

Dr. Hwang faked the cloning research but also the more important stem-cell findings. There were also other ethical questions about how the Koreans obtained eggs—which were not readily available in the local supermarket—for the experiment. This question also flagged violations from other scientists.

Previously, the falsifying of scientific data was the specialty for salesmen on TV or the writers of labels on bottles of fat-reduction products, but now it has become a common occurrence as fraudulent scientists fabricate research for glory or fame.

Admittedly, many moral questions remain about the future of cloning, and no doubt some lowlife scientist will experiment with a human clone, regardless of the ethics or the possible horribly deformed outcome. The world may see a duplicate Osama Bin Laden or Attila the Hun. Sometimes one is plenty.

DUMB SCHMUCKS

THE ACLU
Go Scrooge yourselves.

It's a good thing Bing Crosby isn't around to see what's happened to Christmas in America. This glorious season is supposed to represent a celebration of diversity and not a clash of disparate civilizations. Sadly, school districts are forbidding the singing of Christmas carols, Nativity scenes are banned in public places, and the annual Christmas sales in malls across America have been renamed "holiday sales."

To all this, we say *feh!*

What's not to like at Christmas? People are friendlier, good music fills the air (most of it written by Jews), and there are usually cookies.

We cannot see how anyone's beliefs—Jew, Muslim, or atheist—are jeopardized by people observing *their* beliefs, particularly if the celebration consists of love, family values, spirituality, and contributing to the alleviation of the plight of the poor and the homeless. Christianity would be rather fragile if its 2,000-plus years of culture and beliefs were threatened by Irving Berlin's "White Christmas," Santa Claus's appearance in department stores, and the hanging of mistletoe. (Eggnog makes us a little nauseous, but why quibble?)

We would be the first to complain if the KKK celebrated a holiday of hate with the exchanging of clean sheets or chestnuts roasting on a burning cross. But until that day arrives, hand us the checkbook, and please turn up the volume on "Jingle Bells."

It disturbs us particularly that Jews in America seem to be involved in the repeal of the Christmas movement. If Christmas is abolished from public display, can the extinguishing of Chanukah, the Jewish Festival of Lights, be far behind?

Finally, the lowlife of our sad tale: the ACLU. This organization is at the forefront of efforts to suppress Christmas. It is also vocal in its criticism of the United States's treatment of terrorists. Surely it is the terrorists who have killed thousands and caused the horrible state of fear in which we live, and *not* Frosty the Snowman.

The ACLU's position is that the Constitution protects pornography but not the display of a public Christmas tree. If they succeed, the only place you could legally visit a Christmas tree would be inside a porn shop.

So on December 25, we'll join the Grinch, Tiny Tim, and Rudolph the Red-Nosed Reindeer himself, to wish everyone who still believes in Santa Claus a very merry Christmas.

Even the ACLU.

DAVID BLAINE
Being a schmuck is no trick.

To tell you the truth, we're not sure who the bigger schmuck is: David Blaine and his *fekockteh* stunts or the people who watch them.

Don't get us wrong; we like magic. You want to saw our mothers-in-law in half, be our guest. You really want to impress them? Pull a rabbit fur coat out of your hat.

But David Blaine doesn't do that old-timey stuff. No, he does "street magic." What is street magic, you ask? Good question. Back in Brooklyn, we thought street magic was putting the garbage by the curb at night and having it gone by the morning. To Blaine it means levitating or biting a quarter in half.

But apparently half-eaten quarters don't pay the bills so well, so Blaine started performing crazy endurance stunts, often on the streets of New York. In 1999, he buried himself alive in a glass coffin for a week outside one of Donald Trump's buildings. Sure, if some magician wants to live in a glass box for a week, and it's okay with the Donald, but we're guessing Donald wouldn't be so generous if a bum cozied up outside Trump Plaza in a cardboard box for 20 minutes. Also, is living in a box for a week so impressive? We once knew a guy who was stuck in a subway car from December 1982 to June 1983.

Then in 2000, Blaine pulled a stunt called "Frozen in Time" where he trapped himself inside a block of ice in the middle of Times Square. Please. Anyone who has ever walked out of a Broadway show in February and tried to get a cab knows there's no trick to that.

And how about the stunt where he tried to upstage Harry Houdini himself by living in a fishbowl full of water for a week and then, at the very end, attempted to set a world record by holding his breath for more than nine minutes while trying to escape from heavy chains? As he told a reporter at the time, either he was going to escape from the chains or drown. Well guess what? He did neither.

As far as we're concerned if you want to starve yourself for a week while sitting on top of the Empire State Building, juggling chainsaws, that's one way to go. But we have a better trick for you.

Disappear.

WARD CHURCHILL
Winston he's not.

One of the main differences between the United States and Great Britain is that all the nitwits across the Atlantic spout their harmless inanities on a corner of Hyde Park in London, while here in America we promote these jerks to tenured professors and pay them $114,000 a year.

A supreme lowlife is Ward Churchill, a professor at the University of Colorado, who gained enormous media attention because of a little essay he wrote entitled "Some People Push Back—On the Justice of Roosting Chicken." The gist of his essay was that 9/11 was a reasonable retribution for America's past actions in Iraq.

His title, by the way, was inspired by Malcolm X's remark on the assassination of JFK, that "it was merely a case of the chickens coming home to roost." Classy stuff. He also appended a line spoken by another "scholar," the actor Laurence Fishburne, whose character in the movie *The Cotton Club* says, "You've got to learn that when you push people around, some people push back."

The insensitivity of the Malcolm X quotes and the banality of the movie line, as any kindergarten teacher can explain, is equivalent to the philosophy of a five-year-old child from whom a toy has just been taken.

Just as this essay was discovered, Ward Churchill was scheduled to speak at Hamilton College, so the school canceled at the last minute, but in a cowardly fashion. The college did not have the guts to say it would not offer this hate-filled and twisted individual a podium to spread his anti-American venom to students. Rather, the school fudged, claiming his appearance was canceled under the convenient lie that it might have caused a safety issue.

For those who can hold their noses long enough to read through Churchill's essay, later expanded into a book, the thought must be, "How in the world could someone whose thinking is so shallow, so patently limited in its ability to understand history, so twisted with hatred, and whose logic is buried in dialectic stupidity, ever be in a position to pass along to students this claptrap as history?"

The fault, in what can be charitably called his analysis, is that he disassociates cause and effect, cherry-picks bits of history, and simply ignores events that preceded or caused the actions. History, according to Ward Churchill, begins at a starting point—any starting point—that supports his beliefs.

For example, in one paper he whines about the Allies in World War II and their "strategic bombing campaign" (the foregoing words are placed in quotation marks by Churchill, in order, we suppose, to emphasize that it was all just a cover-up for a scheme of wanton destruction). The war beheld many bombing attacks against Germany and its cities from 1940 to surrender in 1945. But Churchill forgets who first bombed civilian populations in that war, conveniently omitting mention of the Nazi bombing in 1939 of Guernica in Spain, or of Rotterdam in 1940. Both cities were similarly defenseless and of no military value.

In addition, when Great Britain entered the war there was an unspoken understanding that London and Berlin would not be bombed. The Nazis soon decided this was a distinct disadvantage and sent bombers over London to remedy the situation. German revisionist historians admit this tactic was a mistake and that the Nazis intended to murder *other* Brits and *not* Londoners. In the end, both capitals were bombed incessantly. Not in dispute is which country first started the coldhearted bombing of civilian populations.

Ward Churchill has also referred to the First Gulf War as a "holocaust" and said of our troops, "It was a performance worthy of Nazis during the early months of the drive into Russia." He has picked up the narrative as if our soldiers were sent to the Gulf for target practice and sunburns. But he overlooks the fact that many in the civilized world supported the United States's efforts against Iraq. Somehow, he sweeps under history's carpet the cause of why our military went into harm's way—the Iraqi army invasion of Kuwait and Saddam Hussein's cruelty and aggression against his own enemies, and the Kurds, which included the use of torture and poison gas.

Referring to September 11, he legitimizes the Arab murderers as "combat teams" and "soldiers." He also notes that the attackers' having "waited so long to do so [kill 3,000 innocent people] is . . . more than anything, a testament to their patience and restraint." He also states that the terrorists "manifested the courage of their convictions." The helpless and innocent victims of that day he refers to as "little Eichmanns."

Who does this guy think he is, Bill Maher?

COURT JESTERS
Sometimes justices are not only blind, they're dumb.

We could have filled a whole book simply with schmucks from the legal profession—prosecutors, defense attorneys, and judges who often make criminals look like geniuses. But here are a few of our favorite legal lowlifes:

Judge Lance Ito (and the O. J. jury). It's not only bad judges, but also bad justice, that sometimes takes place in our nation's courts. Unfortunately, a peek into the heart of American jurisprudence during the O. J. Simpson trial, brought an unsatisfactory look at both judge and jury.

First of all, to be picked for this jury, a prospective juror had to have the IQ of a matzo ball. To answer all the questions that both lawyers posed, someone could only have been considered for selection if the week before they had received a full frontal lobotomy, or were released from a lunatic asylum. For others, qualification for jury selection might have come because they had gone cold turkey off their meds.

The prosecution and defense lawyers asked prospective jurors the key question to determine the ability to hear the evidence fairly and without bias. Simply, that question was, "Have you ever heard anything about this case before?" Many answered, "No, never."

Let's review this response. From the moment the grisly double murder of a famous athlete's wife appeared in the media, and for months aired on every radio and television news program in the nation, and also as the lead headline in every American newspaper, and with photographs splashed across the front cover of magazines for months, all leading up to that ill-fated day of worldwide television coverage of the white Bronco driving south on I-5 with the entire L.A. police department lined up behind it; and when television sets had been disinfected so they could be brought into hospital operating rooms, and in hellholes in prisons inmates were allowed to listen on transistor radios; and when there were round-the-clock media comments by every pundit and legal analyst in the world; and finally when the newest edition of the board game Clue was rushed to market so people could say, "It was O. J. with the knife in front of his ex-wife's house," it was impossible to understand how anyone not floating on an iceberg in the Bering Sea could claim truthfully that they had never heard a word about this case. This was the ultimate lie of all time. It was as though we asked these same people if they had ever seen the sun? And they responded, "No, not me. I never saw it ever. Maybe once a long time ago." These were the kinds of lowlife jurors picked to sit in judgment at the trial.

Then of course, there was the judge, Lance Ito. Judge Ito had a right to sequester the jurors but he kept them locked up for a month and a half without any contact with their spouses. Could a healthy person concentrate on the trial without wondering about the scheduling of a conjugal visit? How could horny jurors sit and remember the difficult presentation of evidence when minds were drifting off to images of outfits from Victoria's Secret or whether the Viagra pill would be split in half?

Did Ito know he was presiding over a case that was a fraud from beginning to end? How he allowed Johnnie Cochran's summation to include the statement that O. J.'s body had no mark on it, and therefore he did not do the stabbings, is beyond our comprehension. If we stabbed you, whose body would show the wound marks? Yours or ours? If we shot you, would they be looking for the bullet in *our* body?

The latest twist in this sorry saga, of course, was that late last year, O. J. himself tried to publish a despicable book in which he offered his theory for carrying out the murders *if he had committed them*.

We hope it makes Judge Ito and the entire jury proud.

Walter Steed: Here's the story of a Utah judge who evidently felt the need to live up to his surname. In 2006, Judge Steed was removed from the bench—where he had served for 25 years, in addition to being a part-time truck driver—after being found guilty of polygamy and violating the state's bigamy law. Apparently, Judge Steed had three fillies in his stable, and that's illegal. Even in Utah.

Donald Thompson. This charming Oklahoma judge was forced from the bench last year for using a penis pump in court. That's right, a penis pump. Apparently, when the bailiff yelled, "All rise," this limp schmuck needed a little help.

According to the affidavit, Thompson exposed himself during three separate cases. Two court employees told investigators that they saw Thompson attach a suction device to his penis, while five jurors reported hearing whooshing sounds, which they thought were coming from either a bicycle pump, a blood pressure cuff, or an air cushion on the judge's chair.

After a search of his courtroom and chambers yielded items that tested positive for seminal fluid, investigators secured a search warrant to obtain a DNA sample from Thompson. He also allegedly shaved and oiled his penis, according to accounts given to state investigators by a clerk, trial witnesses, and a court reporter. If convicted of the indecent exposure counts, Thompson could face a maximum of 10 years in prison on each charge.

The whole disgusting episode gives new meaning to the phrase, "Here comes da judge."

INTERNET ADDICTS
Visit www.whataschmuck.com.

It is now estimated that 69 percent of all Americans are connected to the Internet and 73 percent have a computer. More impressive than that, we think, is that 90 percent of people over 60 have no idea how to use one. And most will never live long enough to figure out how to hook up a mouse. You want to go online? You have to develop a meaningful relationship with a 15-year-old. Which, if you're not a priest, can be difficult.

Ever talk to someone after they bought a new computer? "We just purchased the *best* one," they brag, "It's the biggest. The smartest."

"What does it do?" we ask.

"We don't know. We only know we bought the best, the biggest, and the smartest." And then the proud couple is quick to add, "We're *so* delighted how useful it is."

"Like doing what?" we ask.

"We don't know but we're planning to take lessons and courses."

"And until then?"

"It stays unopened in the box."

Then someone will usually add, "My nephew is a computer expert and he'll come over to tell me what to do with it."

"When is that?"

"I don't know. He hacked into the IRS computer and he's doing time in Leavenworth."

For the moment and for years later, it's sufficient—almost preferable—that people own a computer without ever having to learn how to install anything or even turn it on. What's important is *telling people* they bought a computer. And also that it's the best one for the lowest price. Since computers are constantly changing and being updated, it is important to own the latest and most modern. So now closets are filling up with unopened boxes of computers.

The expensive purchase at least silenced kibitzer friends who no longer taunt, "You don't have a computer? What kind of a dumb schmuck are you?"

And then you find someone who's got a high-speed Internet connection and he brags, "I can read 3,000 newspapers a day from every country in the world."

We ask, "When's the last time you ever read more than *two* papers a day?"

"Never. But I like the *idea* that 3,000 papers are available to me worldwide and I don't even have to pay for them."

Imagine if, decades ago, the computer came first and the world could have learned information only by gazing at the monitor. Then one day someone invented a newspaper. What would everyone say? "This newspaper invention is amazing. What an improvement over the computer. I can't imagine why no one thought of it before. It even works without electricity. This is what I call progress. For fifty cents a day, I can read about the world.

"And there's more. This newspaper is portable. I can take it with me to read in restaurants and carry it on the plane. I can even take it to the toilet, which is something I could never do with a computer." Think about it; you never hear someone say, "I'm going to the toilet, and I'm taking my laptop."

And when it's the dog's turn to go, which would you rather have to clean up after him, a newspaper or a Macintosh?

And then there are the people who own computers who tell you how every day they're meeting strangers online. They crow, "What a fantastic day. Today, I met hundreds of strangers."

We're quick to question, "Is this your new ambition in life? To meet strangers? Think, schmuck: Before the Internet, did you ever sit in a bus or a ballpark, and say, 'I'd like to meet lots of strangers?' Did you ever enter a restaurant and instead of moving to an empty table go to the one with a man sitting alone and say, 'Hi, stranger, mind if I sit down?'" The truth is, people hate strangers. We go out of our way to avoid them.

From an early age onward, parents advise their daughters, "Don't talk to strangers." But now these women are in chat rooms and every day it's, "Hi, sailor."

If you dial a wrong number on the phone, do you say, "Hey, stranger, don't hang up. We'll chat." No, you slam the receiver down.

When you walk into an elevator with strangers, do you talk to anyone? Everyone stares at the ceiling, looks at their watches, or at the numbers flashing above the door, waiting anxiously for their floor. If one guy smiles at the group, you think he's an escapee from Bellevue, and meanwhile someone else is pressing the emergency bell and calling the police.

It's no different in your apartment building; you pass the same couple in the hallway for 20 years without so much as a hello. You never talk to them. Why? Because they're strangers. If you are about to leave your apartment and hear neighbors in the hall, you wait and don't open the door until they enter the elevator or go into their apartment.

But the strangers you meet on the Internet? Them you give your Social Security number to, a few naked photos, and you invite them over to your apartment for coffee and cake.

And let's face it, the computer has made life harder for everyone.

Take airline reservations. In the old days, you dialed and talked to a real person who said, "Hello, I'm Sue. How can I solve your air travel problems today?" The phone call took 90 seconds and you could book two seats to London in a flash.

Today when you dial the airline, the phone system is computerized and offers more than a thousand options to choose from with menus and submenus. The annoying robotic voice tells you to: "Press 1 for First Class; press 2 for Second Class; press 3 if you have No Class. Press 4 if it's a domestic flight, press 5 if it's international, or press 6 if you don't know geography. Press 7 for the regular meal, 8 for vegetarian, 9 for the kosher meal, and 10 if you wish to donate the meal to World Hunger." By the time you have finished pressing the buttons, the plane has left the airport.

The list of choices on the telephone goes on and on. At last, 10 minutes have passed until a real person answers and says cheerily, "Do you know you could have saved time by making this reservation online?"

ZACARIAS MOUSSAOUI
You can call me Al Qaeda . . .

This lowlife, you may recall, is believed to be the so-called "20th hijacker" in the 9/11 attacks. Twentieth stooge is more like it. Like the other suicide bombers, Zacarias Moussaoui trained at the Oklahoma flight school for his despicable mission. Unlike them, he failed his training and left without a pilot's license.

Moussaoui was arrested in August 2001, a few weeks before the attacks, and indicted three months later. If the reason behind his trial wasn't so deadly serious, the whole affair might have actually been somewhat comical. For starters, Moussaoui declined to work with his court-appointed counsel and opted to represent himself. (The old joke says that a lawyer who represents himself has a fool for a client. Even Saddam Hussein knew to get himself a couple of attorneys. And when they were killed, a couple more.)

Throughout the trial, this French-Moroccan crackpot admitted to things he wasn't even accused of—including that he was working in connection with "shoe bomber" Richard Reid. The fact that this contradicted his previous nutjob testimony didn't seem to trouble Moussaoui at all. "You're allowed to lie for jihad," he said in court. "You're allowed any technique to defeat your enemy."

He also resorted to some sticks-and-stones name-calling that would make a bratty kindergartner feel foolish. In his testimony, Moussaoui would refer to the "United Sodom of America" or the "United Satan of America" or "Slave of Satan John Ashcroft." Clever stuff.

Then midway through his trial, Moussaoui (who by then had realized he needed some legal counsel) surprised the court and pleaded guilty to all the charges against him. And subsequently proceeded to deny that he had any involvement with the 9/11 attacks. Though he was eligible for the death penalty, the U.S. government didn't seek it. Instead, he was sentenced to life in prison and is now serving time in a maximum security Colorado penitentiary.

But that's not the punch line to this story. A few weeks after Moussaoui was sentenced, a voice recording purported to be Osama Bin Laden surfaced in which he denied that this Fredo Corleone of terrorists had anything to do with him. Bin Laden stated that Moussaoui "had no connection at all with September 11. . . . I am the one in charge of the 19 brothers and I never assigned brother Zacarias to be with them in that mission. . . . Since Zacarias Moussaoui was still learning to fly, he wasn't number 20 in the group, as your government claimed." In other words, thanks for nothing.

We can only hope that each of his six consecutive life sentences is more miserable than the next.

RAY NAGIN
What color is your hate?

In 1964 after the U.S. Congress passed the Civil Rights Act, Lester Maddox used an axe handle to drive blacks away from his Pickrick restaurant. In 2006, Ray Nagin, mayor of New Orleans, used his tongue like an axe handle to drive whites away from the ruined gem of a city, when he announced that it was God's will that the Big Easy be forever "chocolate."

And what better day for a racist and hypocrite to make such provocative statements than on Martin Luther King Jr. Day. Nagin, too, had a dream—only in his vision, he imagined an entire southern city inhabited by African Americans without even having to post a "Whites Keep Out" sign.

In 1958, George Wallace, after an unsuccessful gubernatorial run against another aggressive southern bigot, famously bragged that in the future "no other son of a bitch ever out-nigger me again." Wallace was true to his word, and in the next election by appealing to his racist constituency, he was elected governor of Alabama. Some time later, Wallace was shot by a white man, and, after his brush with death, was reborn. He publicly and loudly rejected his bigoted past, an action akin to taking off the KKK robes—but only placing them as far away as his attic.

It appears that Mayor Nagin is taking a chapter from this recent

American history, because in facing the serious challenge to his office that exists in the wake of Hurricane Katrina, he has decided to solidify his black voting base by sending the message that he favors black ethnicity. Nagin also proudly asserted, "This city will be a majority African-American city. It's the way God wants." If this is the way "God wants" then something is wrong, since, presumably, the same God for 200 years made the South a cesspool of slavery.

However, Nagin has not apprehended the economic consequence of this tasty delight—his "Chocolate City." Perhaps Mayor Nagin wishes to start a trend to rename cities in America based on their demographic breakdown. Gary, Indiana, more than 85 percent black, could be called the Cup of Cocoa with Floating Miniature White Marshmallows City. And Saint Louis, at about 50 percent for each race, could be the Black and White Cookie City.

To find a proper name for your city, contact Mayor Nagin who can offer other designations of black and white food or drink combinations along the lines of chocolate-chip cookies, brownies with lightly colored nuts, White Russian or Black Russian vodka and Kahlua drinks, black linguine with octopus ink, or chocolate mousse.

Following such a natural disaster, isn't the idea to build as much consensus as possible? Wouldn't the people of New Orleans be better served if Mayor Nagin followed the extraordinary example of Mayor Rudy Giuliani after 9/11 and worked to bring in leadership (and money) from all communities? Can he even imagine what will happen if New Orleans's white business base does not return to help fund the infrastructure and offer employment to people of all races?

Beyond the money, did the mayor grasp that members of the predominantly white U.S. House of Representatives would have a tough, if not impossible, sell to their constituents to pay for and subsidize a revitalized New Orleans that was striving not for ethnic diversity but for a very un-American racial imbalance?

The negative response to Nagin's bigoted remarks came immediately from both whites and blacks. One Web site began selling a picture of Nagin in a Willy Wonka top hat above the caption, "Willy Nagin and the Chocolate Factory."

In a pitiable effort to deflect the onslaught of criticism of his tasteless remark, Nagin tried to describe that chocolate was made with milk, thereby dissolving the 33 percent of New Orleans's native whites into the visibly chocolate mix.

Unfortunately Nagin only apologized for the callousness of his remark. He did not understand the baseness of these racist and divisive comments. His actions showed he was clueless to the real fact that these destructive words hurt *all* the people of New Orleans.

Alexander Pope said, "At every word a reputation dies." The truth is that Ray Nagin didn't enjoy such a terrific reputation *before* Katrina, and although we can ascribe a large part of the New Orleans debacle to FEMA for its incompetence and inefficiency, the public official who was closest to the chaos and death of downtown and the Superdome was the mayor. His moronic position stated that the buck stopped with FEMA or the brain-dead Louisiana governor Kathleen Blanco, but not with him. He was the guy who simply walked off when the fire started, and blamed everybody else for not putting out the firestorm. Nagin couldn't supervise the overflow of a bathtub. The mayor of Atlantis was more of an expert on flooding.

Meanwhile, less than a year after Katrina, New Orleans went back to the polls for a mayoral election. Surely, we thought, the people will give themselves a chance at rebirth and vote this schmuck out. Shows what we know. Nagin was reelected to office after a tight—and not surprisingly—racially divisive battle.

During the campaign, Nagin promised that if elected, he would develop a "100-day plan" to revitalize New Orleans. Apparently, the mayor was too busy with his chocolate recipes because more than 100 days after taking office again, no plan emerged.

Perhaps the most despicable thing to come out of this lowlife mayor's mouth, though, is something that hits closer to home for us. Two months after he won reelection, Nagin appeared on *60 Minutes* to discuss the rebuilding of New Orleans. When it was suggested by the interviewer that not a lot of progress had been made, Nagin offered a vile comeback that made reference to the site of the former World Trade Center. "You guys in New York can't get a hole in the ground fixed and it's five years later," Nagin snapped. "So let's be fair."

Ground Zero is just a hole in the ground? Funny, that's exactly where we'd like to recommend putting Mayor Ray Nagin.

THE NATIONAL ENDOWMENT FOR THE ARTS
Liberally lying.

The wealthy Hollywood liberal community has long complained about what it perceives as unwarranted censorship of the National Endowment for the Arts. These left-wing show business millionaires bitch and moan that the Washington-based institution has tilted rightward, ideologically controlled by conservatives who believe that any art more racy than Norman Rockwell's *Saturday Evening Post* covers is unsuitable for America's eyes.

Nonsense.

The National Endowment for the Arts was established by Congress in 1965. Since then it has awarded grants to deserving American artists and museums. It sponsors many worthwhile programs: the Jazz Masters, Great American Voices, and Shakespeare in American Communities.

However in the past, it has also awarded grants to regional museums that sponsored exhibits of controversial subjects, including Robert Mapplethorpe's homoerotic photographs at the Corcoran Gallery of Art in Washington, D.C. and Andres Serrano's *Piss Christ* painting, mounted at North Carolina's Southeastern Center for Contemporary Art.

These shocking exhibitions engendered an outcry about the inappropriate use of taxpayer funds, which resulted in Congress inserting a decency clause in NEA guidelines that stipulated "obscenity without artistic merit, is not protected speech, and shall not be funded."

A group of artists, including performance artist Karen Finley, sued the NEA for violating their constitutional and statutory rights by improperly, in their opinion, denying them applications for grants for reasons that their art lacked "decency." The case reached the Supreme Court, which, with commonsense wisdom, struck down the applicants' petition thusly: "[N]either is the Court persuaded that . . . the language of §954(d)(1) itself will give rise to the suppression of protected expression."

Karen Finley complained the loudest that her First Amendment rights were being denied, maintaining that she should have received government funds to mount her one-woman show. The performance featured the smearing of chocolate over her nude body—which, as far as we're concerned, is a waste of perfectly good chocolate. On the other hand, if somebody is willing to pour some ice cream, whipped cream, and a few nuts, we might have the beginnings of a one-woman sundae.

But enough about dessert toppings and artistic freedom. If those rich Democrats in show business voiced true outrage at the lack of funding for the Karen Finleys of the world, you could never tell it by the largesse of their artistic funding. When was the last time any liberal hotshot sponsored a controversial artist along the lines of Mapplethorpe or Chris Ofili, the English painter who used elephant dung as his medium? The answer lies somewhere between never and not in our lifetime.

The loudest Hollywood outcry came from actors who make many millions a picture. But if these Hollywood art connoisseurs offer to correct the NEA funding regulations, then they should cough up some millions of their own. If they unloaded some of the cash, we would not need a taxpayer-subsidized organization. Then, after some avant-garde painter uses the contents of her cesspool in her *oeuvre*, let's see which of those movie magnates buys it and hangs that stinky work in their Beverly Hills family room.

But don't hold your breath.

RESTAURANT CRITICS
Talk about food and whine.

Food critics changed forever dining out from a pleasant, non-challenging, no-nonsense family gathering to a fancy-schmancy, status-conscious event where you had to have spent a year at Berlitz to understand the menu.

Waiters turned into poets, describing the dishes as "The lamb is boiled in a reduction of Australian beetle juice, and then is basted with a turkey gizzard mélange and lovingly caressed by an open flame for 30 seconds before being bathed in a 1946 crapola red wine which is assertive without being impertinent."

Suddenly, Da Bella Gypolla, our local Italian restaurant, became a "ristorante" and overnight, spaghetti became pasta, cheese transformed into *formaggio,* and every shmo diner started using the phrase *"Al dente, per favore."*

In restaurants, the bigger the plate, the smaller the portion. The people love it this way, since they believe they are dining in the continental style. Interested in seeing the meat? Move the mushroom aside.

The ultimate phony restaurant experience, of course, is sushi. Answer this question: Did anyone in the United States eat raw fish *before* it was called sushi? Can you recall anyone who said, "I used to order fish fried, boiled, broiled or pan roasted, but my heart's real desire was to eat chunks of it raw?" Did homemakers heave a big filet of freshly gutted scrod on the dining table and say, "Here's a piece of fish that I forgot to cook. Enjoy."

The truth is, the idea of sushi was probably brought to America by two Jewish businessmen who said, "How can we open a restaurant without the expense of a kitchen, stove, or cooks?"

And by the way, nobody knows what the word "sushi" means anyway. Our bet is that a rough translation describes the American patrons who shell out money to eat dead raw fish—in other words, "schmuck."

Another ridiculous cuisine trend that restaurant critics have spoon-fed us is Cajun food. Hollywood movies routinely depict the dingy, depressing swamp country of southern Louisiana, areas that look so primitive, gloomy, and dark that no sensible person visited there. What food offering could possibly come from such a dank and ominous place? The answer: burnt fish! Or, as it's known on fancy menus: *blackened fish.*

All of a sudden, because restaurant critics told us so, people started thinking that a burnt entree was tasty—never mind that when you do it to meat it's often the first step toward your getting cancer. But smart chefs knew that if they could sell the gullible public on the idea that burnt food was good—especially cheap, bottom-dwelling catfish that were usually thrown away or used for bait—they would not only make more money, but they would also avoid the stress of preparing food rare, medium, or well done. The cooks could throw the fish into a pan, and set the flame to blacken.

It's odd, but nobody eats a burnt bagel. The fad has stayed mainly in the fish area. But, as this concept becomes trendier, we envision the Cajun bagel, burnt to a crisp.

Growing up, our mothers were terrible cooks—they burnt the fish and every other dish just about every night. Who knew that as we chewed on these incinerated pieces of fish, meat, noodle pudding, etc. we were years ahead of the hip food craze?

More Fishy Stories

The burnt Cajun food fad spawned the next phony-baloney restaurant trend—branding the name of the fish to quadruple the menu price. Suddenly, one word placed in front of the fish species was worth another $30 a portion. The two prime examples: *Ahi* tuna and *Chilean* sea bass.

In Ahi tuna (yellow fin), the lowlife phoniness of sushi and burnt Cajun food came together like a perfect storm. In fancy dining places, a patron can choose two different types of tuna—Ahi tuna pieces or tuna tartare, raw tuna sent through a grinder. If you bought a piece of yellow fin at the sushi bar, it would cost you about $14.00 for two pieces, but after taking 12 seconds to be chopped into tartare, and having a sprig of parsley added on top as decoration, it costs $38.50.

If you ordered the Ahi tuna cooked, the price might be $23.00 a portion. But if you preferred to have it "seared" (and strangely, no other fish, fowl, or hoofed animal is ever seared, unless it stands too close to the stove), it ran $47.00.

Similarly, Chilean sea bass benefited from a clever rebranding of its real name: Patagonian toothfish. Who would ever order a "toothfish"— let alone one from Patagonia? (Naturally, if you ever do order this fish, be sure to have it seared.) Incidentally, if you ever looked a Patagonian tooth-fish in the eye, it would be an unforgettable experience and one that redefines the word "ugly." Your brother-in-law looks like George Clooney compared with this prehistoric monstrosity.

Oddly, Americans who eat fish always voice a hesitation: "I hope it doesn't taste fishy." The ultimate praise we make about a piece of fish or any food we're afraid to eat is that it tastes like chicken. Every horrible food offering from ostrich meat to rattlesnake is made acceptable because people say, "It tastes like chicken."

Meanwhile, an entire chicken is only five bucks, but some pretentious schmucks would rather eat something that "tastes like chicken" for $40 a serving.

Of course, it's not only about fish. Food critics and restaurants have convinced us that we ought to pay big money for bitter-flavored European salad vegetables with exotic names, like arugula, radicchio, escarole, fennel, and kale. The pricing was determined by a simple method: the more unpleasant it tasted, the more it cost.

The nagging problem became how to make a bundle from these vegetables. The idea of rebranding these salad ingredients was immediately tossed—which is why we never see Ahi arugula or Chilean fennel on the menu. The ingenious solution was to charge a steep price for the vegetable *alone* but to double the cost if it appeared in a *mélange* of *legumes*. By mixing in kale with the radicchio and other shrubbery, the price soared sky high.

And now we come to dessert—the ultimate restaurant rip-off. A small piece of ice with some sweet food coloring should cost less than a nickel but when it's offered as *sorbet*, it costs $23. Sorbet is supposed to cleanse the palate but the only thing it cleans out is the wallet.

A generous portion of chocolate pudding at the truck stop diner will run about $1.95. But pump air into the pudding, call it mousse, and it's almost time to cash in that 401(k).

A big bunch of red grapes costs $2.85 at the supermarket. At the high-end Italian restaurant, the waiter puts one red grape through a pill-slicing machine to divide it into four pieces. Then, he takes out a pencil-thin food liner, draws a red sugary squiggle around and through the grape sections to make the plate resemble a game of tic-tac-toe. The price on the menu is $35 for this artistic creation called *Uva Caravaggio*.

Where do we think all of this food pornography began? We blame

Craig Claiborne, the former food critic for the *New York Times,* who set the stage for the hundreds of thousands of cooking books that annually infect bookstores. People used to buy dirty books and magazines to look at the pictures. Now they buy cookbooks for their photographs. One day a smart guy will put the two together and make a fortune—Paris Hilton licking a mousse.

CINDY SHEEHAN
Mother doesn't always know best.

Cindy Sheehan is the mother of a deceased soldier, U.S. Army Specialist Casey Sheehan, a Humvee mechanic who died in Iraq in April 2004. The nation's heart went out to the parents of this brave man who volunteered to serve his country and died in defense of freedom.

However, Cindy Sheehan turned her son's death into a national crusade against the war in Iraq. Misguided though it might be, would that her motive were based on some philosophy or moral principle. Sadly, the truth is she exploited a personal tragedy for her own public aggrandizement, trying time and again to extend her 15 minutes in the limelight.

Mrs. Sheehan omitted from her complaints about President Bush that in Tacoma, Washington, in June 2004, he met with and offered personal condolences to her and to other military families at a meeting that, wisely, he chose to keep private. Mrs. Sheehan was the only bereaved person at the meeting who felt the president had not demonstrated proper respect. This imagined, or perhaps invented, personal affront stewed for a year or so until she erupted on the scene as the liberal media's Mother Courage.

Acting like some offended third world potentate, she then demanded a powwow with the president at his Crawford, Texas, ranch.

Needless to say, it's a ridiculous precedent for the nation's Chief of State to offer private chitchats to every disgruntled or unhappy citizen—even one who has lost a child in a war. (But just in case he has some time next month, there are a couple of tax bills we received that we would like to sit down and discuss with Mr. Bush, not to mention the miserable post-woman who never drops off the mail before 1:00 P.M.)

We believe that this mother insults the sacrifice her son and many others have made in Iraq. At the same time, her blind and uninformed criticism of the war undermines the efforts of her son's fellow soldiers—many of whom must wish she would shut up since she has nothing of substance to add.

It's time for whoever is directing Cindy Sheehan (Michael Moore? The Democratic National Committee?) to give one more instruction—"exit stage left."

TV WEATHERMEN
What a disaster.

On a slow news day, local television stations employ a ratings-boosting technique. It's a day when no pretty, young white American women are murdered, there are no high-profile child abductions, no bird flu pandemics, no outbreaks of mob violence, and no celebrity divorces. The station manager instructs the weather staff to look around for an attention-grabbing story. The staffers look into past rating-boosters and then announce to the public, "Stay tuned for the worst storm of the century."

The storm may be a tiny speck on some wave in the middle of the Indian Ocean, but it may definitely be coming our way, and if not definitely, at least possibly, and the smidgen on the map may turn out to be a real storm, but if it doesn't, it won't be, but the surf fishing will definitely be affected.

To add some drama, the station waits until the regular programming begins so that they can interrupt it with a bulletin to warn about the storm. The announcer doesn't know exactly when it's arriving, so the station writes a teaser crawl under the picture that reads, "Big killer storm may be heading our way later. Stay tuned for exclusive coverage."

The weather reporter says, "The storm could be here by 9:00 P.M. Or maybe 10:15. Possibly, at the very latest, by 11:00 P.M. unless the winds die down and then the storm won't arrive until after midnight but that would be only in certain parts of the metropolitan area." Which parts? Nobody knows.

At first, the report indicates that it's not too dangerous but a second glance from the panel of weather experts suggests that it could be the most damaging storm on record. Their advice: You must stay tuned to see how this storm develops. If you take even 30 seconds to go to the toilet, you could miss what happens and die.

Frightened viewers stay glued to the station, waiting for a second-by-second update on this storm that's heading into the area. This new information will give them the edge in case of devastating tornado winds, flash flooding, or a 22-foot accumulation of snow and ice.

The people at home are worried to death and will not budge from the living room. They realize that unless they stock up on batteries, bottled water, canned food, and other essentials, they will be trapped in the dark without food, water, or condoms.

It becomes an apparent life-and-death decision to make, either rush to the store and face the height of the storm, or stay home, do nothing, and starve. Woe to those people with elderly mothers who receive a hot meal on a daily basis. Maybe it's possible to order take-out Chinese food for Mom because it's too risky to go out and everyone knows that Chinese take-out food would be delivered even if it was ordered in the midst of an air raid. We always wondered, if all the Chinese restaurants on Sundays are filled with Jews, in China on Sundays, are all the Jewish restaurants filled with Chinese?

You wait for more updated information about the oncoming weather phenomenon, which the weatherperson will not definitely categorize as a hurricane, tornado, squall, cyclone, twister, gale, blizzard, thunderstorm, snowstorm, or tempest.

Then whatever it is, the storm seems to be growing worse but this always happens far away from where we live. Outdoors the sun is shining but the meteorologist says it could change in an instant.

To prepare for the worst, you close the windows and the doors; turn off the air-conditioning, so you're sweating inside and hungry.

The time of arrival of this storm and its size are not definite. It could be here soon, later, or not at all. It might be small, medium, or large. The station doesn't know for sure but don't turn the channel because when it does, you will be the first on the block to know.

Then, despite all the weather warnings, nothing happens. The television station offers no apology. Instead, it tells you the reasons—all out of its control—why the storm veered at the last minute and went out to sea, or made a U-turn on Bruckner Boulevard in the Bronx and was last seen heading to Uzbekistan.

But, stay tuned. Who knows when the next storm is coming?

For the most part though, when we watch the weather on television, the only concern is if tomorrow will be hot or cold, sunny or rainy, and that's it! Should we wear a light coat if it's chilly or heavy coat if it's cold? If it rains, what time in the day will it begin and will it be heavy or light? This information should take 40 seconds to deliver.

But television stations have to fill 30 minutes of airtime and stretch the weather report into 5 boring minutes. So, the weatherman will provide as much useless information as possible to fill in the time.

Did we say weatherman? We meant *meteorologist*. Meteorologists are television announcers with a college degree. The degree allows them to listen to weather reports on another television station, be referred to as "Doctor," and point on a map as if they were General Eisenhower plotting troop movements on D-Day.

A meteorologist will advise you that the storm is coming, how it began as a mild breeze from a broken fan in the country of Gabon in equatorial Africa, picked up power over Alaska, and then strengthened somewhere over the plains of Alberta, Canada, swept into the United States, circling the Midwest in the odd shape of a pretzel, turned east in Ashtabula, Ohio, and arrived in Philadelphia where it sat like a matzo ball in thick broth for the weekend before it picked up steam and headed to New York City. We thought we were listening to a weather report, when instead it was a lesson in world geography.

How is all this information helpful to you? It's not. After each weather report, you ask, "Who's interested in this garbage?" The answer may surprise you: other weather reporters. But it's a waste of time to an old Jewish woman trying to leave the house to buy a knish and not knowing if she should take an umbrella, a sweater, or whether the wheels of her walker will be stuck in the slush.

The weather people recite statistics about the wind: it's high, it's low, or it's midland. And then the direction of the wind: it's north by southeast but it may change to west by due south around 3:00 P.M. with the chance of altering course to east by southwest later in the day. Did you ever consider, "What's the direction of the wind? I'm going to the delicatessen and must plot the route on my compass to avoid the direction of the oncoming wind?"

Temperature is another fact stretched into a long monologue of worthless data. The weather map doesn't reveal the temperature where *you* live; it always shows the temperature at the airport. Who lives at the airport? Then the weatherman announces the temperature of surrounding towns like Rockville Center, Copake Lake, or Maplewood. You don't live in these places either. The station mentions these locales so the next day some schmuck will show up at the local diner and brag, "Our town was on the weather report last night."

Temperature in Celsius or Fahrenheit? Who knows the difference? And if you do know, who cares?

The report publicizes the various times and places of the tides. Is it a high tide? Or a low tide? What do you care about tides? Do you keep a boat in the living room?

Weatherpeople are imprecise. The guesses are always in percentages. There's an 80 percent chance of rain. A 12 percent possible chance of sleet. Maybe, a 46 percent chance of a tsunami. Either they know or they don't. What should we do, bring 80 percent of an umbrella or 43 percent of a raincoat?

But the weather folk provide more insignificant nonsense: the barometric pressure. When have you thought, "It's life or death that I know the barometric pressure?" Would you miss not knowing it? Have you heard anyone say, "I'm not leaving this building because of the barometric pressure." Or, did friends ever call you and say, "We're canceling the bar mitzvah because the barometer is rising?"

Then there is the almighty Doppler weather map! The Doppler map is a confusing adaptation of radar weather photographs. In the afternoon at 4:00 P.M., a surprise downpour drenches you. Later, on the 6:00 P.M. news, the weatherman shows the green or yellow or blue clump of rain mass as the showers moved earlier through your city. Better than the Doppler photo would be to show you soaked to the skin and cursing the weatherman. Have you ever been asked, "Say, last night, wasn't that a vibrantly colored Doppler map?"

Perhaps the most annoying weather fact is the double degree readings. The weatherman says, "Today, the temperature is 23 degrees, but with the wind chill factor it will be 9 degrees." Either it's 23 or 9 degrees. How can you dress for 23 and 9 degrees at the same time? You can't. So you go outside and then you think, "I feel 23 but with this wind chill factor I'm suddenly feeling 9."

The wind chill reading is like saying it's raining, but without the rain, it's dry.

We can say with 100 percent certainty—you're all schmucks.

SCHVITZY SCHMUCKS

BARRY BONDS
A Giant among schmucks.

Despite centuries of amateur athletes pursuing the noble Olympic motto of *Citius, Altius, Fortius* (Faster, Higher, Stronger), modern-day athletes numbering many lowlifes—earning mega millions and more—swear by a new sports motto: *Cheat, Lie, Bulk Up.*

If a man walks around for three days with an erection, he will usually announce it's because of a Viagra pill and not some penile muscle spasm coupled with thinking 24-hour supererotic thoughts. But when an athlete goes from being a skinny wimp to the Rock of Gibraltar, he will swear on a stack of contracts that it was all due to extensive weight training and nutritional supplements. That is, until the day when his urine tests positive for steroids.

We think that Barry Bonds, arguably the best baseball player in history, was, to mix a sports metaphor, skating on thin ice when he testified that he did not know his trainer handed him steroid creams and pills. He believed these were nutritional supplements and flaxseed oil. Bonds must have been too muscular between his ears not to realize that nutritional supplements and flaxseed oil do not come in druggist's prescription bottles or in unmarked envelopes.

The parade of professional players admitting they used steroids or other performance-enhancing drugs appearing before a House committee, made for an ugly picture of American sports. On display was a lineup of baseball players, mostly home run kings with cartoonlike upper-body strength, who testified (some, under immunity) about not taking steroids and other, performance-enhancing drugs.

Foremost among this pumped-up crowd was 40-year-old Rafael Palmeiro (3,000 hits and 500 homers), who pounded his fist like it was Nikita Khrushchev's shoe and proclaimed, "I have never used steroids." Five months later, he tested positive and was suspended for 10 days. His alibi? "It was an accident." If a car hits you, providing it is not your wife driving the car, that's an accident. But it's hard to believe you can take performance-enhancing drugs for more than four years, have muscles that have muscles, and still claim the look occurred by accident. Also, wouldn't you notice your head getting bigger and your testicles disappearing?

Another cretin in that congressional murderer's row was admitted steroid abuser Jose Canseco, who used the hearing to plug his new autobiography. In various interviews on the subject, Canseco swung wildly claiming that 50 to 85 percent of baseball players also used steroids. If this was true, now is the time to load up on drug company stock. Canseco never had to face a teary disillusioned, seven-year-old boy in love with America's great pastime, asking, "Say it ain't so, Jose."

ESPN took the story even further and collected photographs of Barry Bonds's career, starting in 1986 when he was a fit, but thin, 185-pound rookie, playing for the Pittsburgh Pirates. In the last picture, Bonds looks as he does today, a super muscular man with an incredible chest and massively powerful arms—and a head that would fit right in at the Macy's Thanksgiving Day Parade.

Bonds added 40 pounds of muscle and increased his home run production dramatically after he turned 35. Prior to that, the most home runs he had hit in one season was 46. In 2001, he hit 73 home runs at age 37. When we turned 37, we were already taking 15-minute naps and thinking about asking our girlfriends to cut up the steak into little pieces in restaurants.

Bonds credited his newly found hitting achievements to an innovative training regimen. If we begin examining the statistics in 1993, when he moved to the San Francisco Giants, his average home runs per at bats start at about 10 percent and continue at about this level until he belted that record-setting 73 home runs and increased his average to 15 percent. It is an amazing feat that we would designate as "Ruthian," if we didn't also have reason to believe that the record was allegedly steroid enhanced.

Perhaps we should coin a new term, "Bondian Bargain," to describe the inner compromise an athlete makes to rise to and to remain on the top of his game no matter what legal or illegal deal he makes.

Personally, we are looking for a steroid that will be like Viagra for the brain. On second thought, who wants to be known as hardheaded?

MARK CUBAN
Giving billionaire loudmouths a bad name.

Have you seen this lunatic on TV? Of course you have. You can't turn on a basketball game anymore without seeing him there on the sidelines in a Dallas Mavericks jersey, screaming at some referee. It wouldn't be so annoying if he were just another crazy fan at a game, but Mark Cuban is the *owner*.

Say what you want about George Steinbrenner and all his *mishegas*, but he would *never* put on Yankee pinstripes and start kicking dirt at an umpire.

So how did Mark Cuban get to be the owner of an NBA team? Simple, he made billions of dollars the new-fashioned way: he started an Internet company. What this company did, no one can say. It might have made something or sold something or tried to sell something or helped people communicate or put dirty pictures of themselves online. What it did isn't the point. The point is that one day, his company *might* do something. In 5 years or 10 years or maybe even sooner if someone else's Internet company does not figure out a way not to do things faster than Cuban's company did not do them. But because Mark Cuban's company might make a dollar in a few years, someone decided to pay him $5 billion to sell it now.

He may be a schmuck, but he's no schmuck. He sold his company and bought a basketball team.

Now, of course, he thinks he's Donald Trump.

Trust us, we know Donald Trump. This guy is no Donald Trump. He doesn't even deserve to be allowed to watch *The Apprentice*! In fact, even *The Apprentice* proved to be too much for Mark Cuban. He tried to rip off Trump's show with a program of his own called *The Benefactor*, but it was canceled midway through the first season.

So now Mark Cuban just goes to Mavericks games and screams at people. He yells so much that every once in a while the NBA gets tired of his loudmouth act and fines him hundreds of thousands of dollars. But instead of jumping up and down and stamping his feet some more about the punishment, Cuban (who has been fined nearly $2 million so far) sends a matching gift to charity. It's hard to criticize that, but, frankly, we'd prefer that he kept his mouth shut and gave twice as much to charity.

About the nicest thing we can say about the man is that he has a cat named Meshugana. It should be the other way around.

THE NCAA

We have a couple of names we'd like to call you.

In April 2006, the NCAA, the organization that governs college sports, banned the use of "hostile" or "abusive" team nicknames or mascots. This decision came a year after the group tried to stop 18 college teams from using long-standing Native American names like Sioux, Seminole, and Chippewa unless those Native American tribes granted permission.

Jackie is particularly sensitive to this problem. For years he traveled America, touring big cities and hundreds of small towns where he was called "Jew bastard" thousands of times—and that was just from the Jews.

We are aware, of course, that some Native Americans would feel embarrassed if their tribal name was used as a derogatory college nickname. We could understand if American colleges had chosen truly hostile and abusive nicknames like the Rampaging Wops, Big Heebs, or the Fighting Colored Folk. But this is not the case with Native American tribes that are, by and large, honored by colleges for their bravery and fighting spirit.

What's next? Will People for the Ethical Treatment of Animals sue to stop the use of bird, bear, dog names for sports teams? Or what about color-blind people? Will they be allowed to sue because they can't actually tell the difference between the Harvard Crimson and the green field? And will the city of Dublin soon be voting on whether to allow Notre Dame to be called Fighting Irish?

And it's not just sports teams. One day garbage men became "sanitation engineers" and "waste management expediters" and no one knew who the hell they were or what they did. The garbage collectors had never once objected to being called garbage men. The attempt at this radical name change came from people on the Left—card-carrying members of the political correctness militia—who decided that the garbage men *should* take offense. (Be honest. Do you say to your spouse, "Honey, it's Thursday, please take out the bags of waste because tomorrow the waste management expediters are coming"?)

These same liberal do-gooders also determined that offensive terminology had to go. One of their most conspicuous defeats came from deaf people who refused to be called hearing impaired. They said, "We are deaf. We cannot hear. Impairment is for people in the process of losing their hearing. We are deaf!" That's the way it has remained, one small victory for common sense and one big defeat for the political correctness police.

The next battle involved blind people, who are not "blind" but are "visually impaired." And what about midgets, who are known simply as "little people"? If they are a bit taller, they are called "vertically challenged." We also had a friend who used to be bald, but is now officially "follicly disadvantaged."

Last year, our good friend Morty suffered pains in his chest and down his arms. The paramedics arrived at his office and he shouted out, "I'm having a heart attack," The head of the EMS team shook her head, and said, "No. That term is politically incorrect. Think again and tell us what's happening to you." Morty, who never intended to become a martyr for any cause no matter how worthy, hastily replied, "Okay, I'm having a *coronary episode.*"

For the past 30 years, we have eaten regularly at a Midtown restaurant and been served by a waiter named Francisco from Ponce, Puerto

Rico. As we usually do, this year we asked him, "Paco, are you going to the Puerto Rican Day Parade?" He scowled at us and replied, "I am not Puerto Rican. I am Latino, or maybe Hispanic." He became another victim of the political correctness battle who has lost his place of birth and also his native pride.

By the way, did you spot the politically incorrect title we gave to Paco's job? There are no waiters or waitresses anymore, only servers, waitpersons, and wait staff. We would once have called the people who spend their lives thinking up these new nongender, politically correct terms nitwits or lunkheads. However, we'll merely call them mentally challenged; but this thought was merely an *idea burst* and not a *brainstorm* because we would never offend epileptics.

Then there are homosexuals. You can't even speak this word it's so politically incorrect. Mention the word "gay" in many states and it's considered a form of harassment. If you identify a man as a homosexual, it's an insult. Even "sexually challenged" is deemed inappropriate.

The truth is that today men and women are proud to be homosexuals. For past years, they were either in the closet, coming out of the closet, looking for closets, or at least redecorating a closet.

And where will it all end? Will we soon see the neutering of classic plays like Eugene O'Neill's *The Iceperson Cometh* or George Bernard Shaw's *Person and Superperson.* And how about cartoons or comic books: Batperson and Robin, Popeye the Sailorperson. With political correctness, the safest bet is to call somebody "Hey You."

As far as we're concerned, the NCAA and every other politically correct schmuck in the world should leave all this name changing to the people who can really benefit from it the most—Jewish comedians.

DEAD SCHMUCKS

YASSER ARAFAT
He broke the West Bank.

I f Yasser Arafat hadn't been a world-class terrorist, he would have made a helluva banker. After all, when he died in 2004, the former Palestinian president's net worth was estimated to be between $300 million and $1.3 billion. Which shows you that you can really save a lot of money by wearing the same shmatte on your head for 40 years.

Looking back, it was clearly not peace the late Arafat wished for—it was a healthy PLO IRA. (Though obviously not a *Roth* IRA.) In fact, if there ever existed a small hope for peace in the Middle East, it was undone by Arafat. He sponsored suicide bombings after the Oslo peace accord when President Clinton and Israel's Prime Minister Barak offered to return much of the disputed territories.

After Oslo, Arafat went back to Palestine a hero and was elected president by an overwhelming 88 percent of the vote. The Palestinians were filled with hope that the repressive violent behavior in the region would come to an end with the handshakes and the comity that came from the Camp David meetings. They were mistaken.

One group noticeably absent from the voting booth back in 1996 was Hamas, the sometime political party and full-time terrorist group that won the 2006 elections in Palestine. One reason for Hamas's defeat of Arafat's Fatah Party was, ironically, the issue of corruption and cronyism.

Maybe in the future, in honor of Arafat's memory, we shall prefer the devil we know in the Middle East. Unlike the radical Muslim leaders amassing power in the region, at least Arafat was smart enough to understand the terrible outcome of an all-out, to-the-death war with Israel. Probably because he had some shekels in Israeli banks.

It is rumored that Arafat's last wish was not to face Mecca but to be buried facing Switzerland so he could always gaze at the millions he'd salted away in Zurich.

CHARLES COUGHLIN
This father didn't know best.

A few weeks after the horrifying events in Germany of November 9 and 10, 1938, when organized thugs destroyed Jewish property and synagogues in what became known as *Kristallnacht* ("The night of broken glass"), one American voice trumpeted a justifiable reason for these unprovoked and murderous Nazi Party–sponsored attacks: "[This] Jewish persecution only followed after Christians were persecuted." Huh? The last Christian persecution that we heard about in which something to do with Jews had involved Romans in bedsheets and some hungry lions.

This remark might have been the expression of somebody who had a day off from a lunatic asylum, or of Nazi propaganda minister Joseph Goebbles (same thing), who routinely aired his hateful views on German radio. But in fact, it was America's own Father Charles Edward Coughlin, an ordained Catholic priest.

For a decade on Sundays, this rabid right-wing hatemonger broadcast virulent anti-Semitism to an audience of 30 million, especially urban Irish Catholics. He was this country's first patron saint of revulsion radio, a vicious demagogue, who, at the height of his enormous popularity, attracted a larger listening audience than President Franklin D. Roosevelt's Fireside Chats.

His prestige derived from being a man of the cloth, his homey native Christianity, and a mellifluous voice that served radio perfectly. Father Coughlin championed the "paranoid style," an effective method of blaming "those people" (Wall Street, international bankers, Washington liberals, commies, labor organizations, and most of all, Jews) for all of the ills that afflicted the economically lower classes of American society.

He feared the threat of worldwide communism and considered the fascist dictatorships of Adolf Hitler and Benito Mussolini as righteous bulwarks against the Bolshevik danger. He was able, cleverly, to marry the American hatred and fear of communism to his own anti-Semitism by coining the term "Judeo-Bolshevik threat." He also incorrectly ascribed a hidden and secret Jewish past to both Lenin and Stalin. Apparently, somebody forgot to tell Stalin about his Jewish connection since he was more anti-Semitic than the Cossacks. His idea of playing polo was using a convenient Jew as the ball.

Coughlin also formed the National Union of Social Justice, which published a nasty little newspaper that reached one million Americans and was sold widely in churches. In that paper he also reprinted *The Protocols of the Elders of Zion,* the infamous forged screed that falsely claimed a clandestine Jewish banking conspiracy dominated the world's markets. (The truth is, if you put two Jewish businessmen in the same room, you don't have a conspiracy—you have a vicious argument, followed by a handshake and a deal.)

Coughlin later changed the name of his organization to the Christian Front, marking one of the first national attempts to exploit the "Christian" name for a repugnant American cause. The Front was just that, a front for an ineffective brownshirt group of hooligans until 1940, when the FBI uncovered a large cache of arms at the New York office along with detailed plans to murder Jews, U.S. communists, labor leaders, and some congressmen and then establish a Hitler-style dictatorship.

In 1938, Father Coughlin led followers in a Manhattan demonstration to protest offering Jews political asylum, chanting, "Send the Jews back where they came from in a leaky boat." and "Wait until Hitler comes over here." Even in 1939, two years before Pearl Harbor, Coughlin questioned America's reasons for entering the European conflict thus: "Must the entire world go to war for 600,000 Jews in Germany?"

His airtime in the United States ended shortly after the invasion of Poland in 1939, when lobbying efforts passed new broadcast rules that limited obviously incendiary speech. To disobey the new standards meant that radio stations would risk losing their valuable licenses, so few did it.

Ironically, if Father Coughlin's shock jock sermons aired today they would likely be lost among all the current radio rage. But for being the first to turn up the volume on such mass media propaganda, we present the good father with the first annual Golden Microphone Award.

And he knows where he can put it.

THE MARLBORO MAN
Where there's smoke,
there's a lawsuit.

David McLean may not be a household name, but his face once sold countless cartons of cigarettes. In the early 1960s, McLean, a rugged television and movie actor, became one of the models to portray the legendary Marlboro Man in commercials and print ads.

In the mid 1980s, McLean developed emphysema and eventually had a tumor removed in 1994—at which point the erstwhile Marlboro Man saddled up and became a vocal antismoking advocate. McLean died of lung cancer in 1995 at the age of 73.

A year after his death, McLean's widow and son sued Philip Morris (the makers of Marlboro) for wrongful death, claiming that while doing the ads, McLean was required to smoke and inhale up to five packs per day in order to present the perfect pose of the gritty, masculine cowboy enjoying a flavorful smoke.

Similarly, another actor/model named Wayne McLaren did some work as the Marlboro Man in the 1970s and he, too, died of lung cancer, at the age of 51. In his last days, McLaren embarked on a public antismoking campaign in the form of a startling television commercial that juxtaposed his handsome cowboy image with photographs of him in the hospital bed wasted and dying. His mother said that some of his last words were "Tobacco will kill you, and I'm living proof of it."

Cigarettes kill you. No doubt. Based on current rates of smoking among the population, estimates are that 25–30 million Americans will die prematurely from smoking-related illnesses in the future.

But people who sue cigarette companies? Well, we think they're just blowing smoke. We ask these venal hypocrites, "Did the cigarette manufacturers cause the cancer or did you *ask* for the cancer?"

Who doesn't know that cigarette smoking causes cancer? Raise your hand. The surgeon general's warning has been on every pack of smokes for the past 40 years. It would be like reading the poison warning on a can of Drano and drinking it anyway. Would you then sue the makers of Drano for the bad taste in your mouth and the loss of your esophageal lining?

Or maybe you take out a kitchen knife and stab yourself in the heart. Does your family then come out and say, "That lousy bastard knife company. Let's go to court to sue those people for killing Uncle Dummy because no warning was printed that stabbing could kill."

As for smoking, once upon a time, we thought it was cool, the height of suavity. No more so than in the most famous cigarette-smoking scene in movie history—1942's *Now, Voyager*, starring Bette Davis and Paul Henreid.

In the film, Henreid's character, Jerry, and Davis's character, Charlotte, realize they are star-crossed lovers who will never be together. They have a sad farewell in which, as a final act of love and intimacy, Jerry lights up *two* cigarettes with one match and offers one to Charlotte. The smoke curls up in front of the couple as they kiss good-bye forever.

Today, whenever we watch this love scene, we wonder how awful their mouths must have tasted of cigarettes, and how their clothes probably smelled horribly of smoke after many takes and retakes. Most of all we wonder whether in real life their health was affected adversely by smoking.

The only fact we do know is that Henreid lived to be 84 and Davis lived until 81 and neither one is on record bringing suit against a cigarette manufacturer.

WALTER O'MALLEY
This one's for Brooklyn . . .

We know people—cultured, refined, and decidedly nonviolent people—who will calmly and sincerely state, "I do not believe in the concept of hell, but if it exists, I hope that Walter O'Malley is there."

O'Malley, the owner of the Brooklyn Dodgers, you may recall, did the unthinkable, the unforgivable: In 1957 he wrenched the team from their native Brooklyn soil (where a team had existed since 1884) and moved the team to Los Angeles. To Brooklynites, the Dodgers's departure represented far more than the transfer of a sports franchise; it sounded the death knell for a vibrant, multicultural borough. More heartbreaking for many young people at that time, it was the first reminder that the world could be a very cruel place, and that once the wheels of commerce started turning, nothing could be done to stop them.

Back in the 1950s, the Brooklyn Dodgers were not just the *other* New York baseball team—a greater case could be made for the New York Giants. Rather, Brooklyn existed in its own loopy and wonderful reality, part of but separate from the turn-of-the-century five-borough union known as New York City. And the Boys of Summer had been constant National League contenders for 10 years, finally winning a World Series victory in 1955 and earning a sure sainthood for left fielder Sandy Amoros.

But his Vatican, Ebbets Field, that small bandbox of a stadium, was aging and O'Malley envisioned a modern, larger ballpark built in a prime location in downtown Brooklyn near convenient subway lines and also near the Long Island Railroad. A canny businessman, O'Malley understood that many of the team's loyal fans had moved to the suburbs but remained faithful.

This is not the place to describe the failed stadium negotiations or to embark on a revisionist argument that New York City power broker Robert Moses was the actual villain. O'Malley robbed the hearts of Brooklyn's fans, and he alone drove the getaway car. Moses, at worst, pointed the direction out of town.

The Brooklyn Dodgers's westward ho–ing signaled the beginning of the coldhearted, make-money-at-all-cost decisions that would perpetuate the game of musical chairs we play with sports franchises to this day. Of no importance was the prior devotion of fans, nor how much money teams had made in previous years. Self-centered and lowlife owners would discard old loyalties like chinked nine irons or first wives.

The New York Giants moved west the following season, up the coast to San Francisco. And nearly 40 years later, in Los Angeles, fans that had never given a second's moment of regret for the theft of the Dodgers, were shocked, *shocked,* when their beloved NFL team, the Los Angeles Rams, moved to Saint Louis.

On second thought, hell is too good for Walter O'Malley. He should have to spend eternity in Saint Louis.

PABLO PICASSO
Color him a schmuck.

In the 19th century, people gazed at paintings, landscapes or portraits, and exclaimed, "What a beautiful rendition of the Hudson Valley!" Or, "Didn't Whistler's mother make an attractive subject arranged in a masterful rendering of classical composition?"

With the arrival of modern art in the 20th century, the phonies came out of the cracks in droves, especially those pretenders that doted on the famed Spanish artist Pablo Picasso.

When you gaze at a Picasso, no one admits, "I don't understand this painting" because friends would assume you have no taste or refinement and, worse, no appreciation for modern art.

God forbid a young man in his twenties should ever confess, "Picasso? My four-year-old niece could paint that!" and their girlfriends would dump them in a minute. So to sound sophisticated to his beloved, the schmuck says he loves Picasso even though he thinks the paintings are garbage. To enhance this deception, he creates a spiel of appreciation, applauding every cockamamy line, the vibrant coloring, the energy and the delicate tones, and the chaotic condition of the world it captures. And if he's a world-class phony, he even admires the frame, noting how it's the perfect one for this painting because Picasso adored knotty pine.

Phonies point to a Picasso painting and explain why the bull's head is on top of the smokestack, why the lampshade is on the side of the goat, why the woman's leg is coming out of the salami, and most notably, why Picasso named the painting *Enchanted Sunset in Sevilla*.

And every phony stands around, nods, and says, "Yes, yes, that is the perfect title."

If your brother-in-law painted a picture like Picasso, he would be locked away in a sanitarium. If we showed you a painting of a banana under a suspension bridge, a spoon protruding from a pig's head, and the moon shining under a sewer grating, you would say, "Who painted this? A serial killer?"

But if we preface the presentation with, "Here's a Picasso." You say, "Picasso! How fascinating! How marvelous! What a masterpiece! All the disparate shapes blend together to express the painter's true artistic meaning."

True story: We have a wealthy friend who owned a Picasso and only when an art expert came to dinner last year, did our friend learn that for the past 30 years, he had been hanging the Picasso upside down.

JEANNETTE RANKIN
All we are saying
is give war a chance.

J eannette Rankin is a name that will live in infamy. The only member of Congress to vote against declaring war on Japan after the attack on Pearl Harbor, Rankin said brazenly at the time, "Killing more people won't help matters."

But unlike the attack on Pearl Harbor, we should have seen Jeannette Rankin's lunacy coming.

Rankin's career began auspiciously enough when she was elected to Congress as a Republican from Montana in 1916, the first woman to serve in either the House or the Senate, and one of the first women to be elected to *any* world governing body. In 1941, she still had a key to the ladies' room at the Capitol.

But after Pearl Harbor—in what seems to be a pathetic and narcissistic attempt to steal some of the limelight from President Roosevelt's war decree—she became the front-page sidebar story in every American newspaper, the sole dissenter to the nation's march to war and our extracting swift moral revenge.

Rankin, however, had been a lifelong pacifist who had vigorously campaigned against any U.S. involvement in wars. In the late 1930s, she had good company in her isolationist views. Charles Lindbergh and the America First Party were active voices for keeping America out of the

European conflict. But even the America Firsters disbanded on December 11, four days after the Japanese invasion (and, incidentally, the day Hitler declared war on *us*, not vice versa), realizing that the United States's only option was war.

Not Jeannette Rankin. Strong-willed and opinionated, she unrepentantly held on to her belief that the United States should never go to war, saying, "As a woman I can't go to war, and I refuse to send anyone else." (And really, who asked her to go? If fighting a war depended on overage, couch potato women and men, there would be no wars.)

Now here's the bizarre part of this tale: Rankin's 1941 sentiment was almost an exact replay of her most unforgettable quote, uttered in April *1917*, after President Woodrow Wilson exhorted the nation to declare war on Germany, stating, "American ships have been sunk. American lives taken, in ways which it has [*sic*] stirred us very deeply."

Congresswoman Rankin's bellicose response to Wilson? "I want to stand by my country, but I cannot vote for war. I vote no."

Jeannette Rankin a schmuck? We vote yes. Twice.

DR. HERMAN TARNOWER
He put the "die" in diet.

There had been other fad weight-loss programs before Dr. Herman Tarnower's famed Scarsdale Diet, but none had ever made much sense to us. And while we should have been skeptical of any diet named after a fancy Jewish suburb, Tarnower's regimen seemed kind of sensible. Four full glasses of water per day? Sure. If you drank enough water there would be no room for food. Plus, it had the added weight-loss benefit of the exercise involved making you run back and forth to the bathroom all day.

Not everyone was a fan of Tarnower, however, and in 1980, he was murdered. Amazingly, he wasn't shot by a hungry patient, but by his lover, headmistress Jean Harris, who discovered that Dr. Tarnower was having a little nosh on the side. It's also possible that he got in her way while she was running to the bathroom.

But even death could not stop Dr. Tarnower from starting a feeding frenzy of fad diets.

Many of those early diets advised against eating fat, and soon federal law mandated that nutrition labels list the fat content of all packaged food items. This gave rise to a multibillion-dollar food industry of items noted for having low fat, no fat, and the dreaded "trans fat." (All across America, wives were soon explaining to their husbands, "I'm not fat, honey. I just look fat. And it's *trans* fat.")

The lack of success of this concept is fairly evident—it is now estimated that 58 million Americans are obese. That tub of frozen yogurt may be fat free, big guy, but perhaps eating 42 of them in one sitting isn't the way to go.

Then one day, like the sudden disappearance of the buffalo, all the fat warnings vanished and were replaced by the good news that fat was in, and the bad news that carbohydrates were out. And because this new fad diet edict came from a physician, Dr. Robert Atkins, it was accepted as medical and scientific gospel.

Essentially, the new diet said a person could eat lots of meat and fat but no carbs—the latter found mainly in bread, potatoes, and pasta. This was the best news for U.S. beef and pork producers since the creation of the bacon cheeseburger. (Which, come to think of it, was a typical Atkins breakfast.) If Dr. Atkins said that carbs were out, could an entire new line of low-carb, no-carb, and perhaps *trans*carb food products be far behind?

What's more, we learned, certain carbs could be consumed at specific times of the day to effect the proper metabolism for maximum weight loss. Soon we heard friends say, "I can't eat this piece of one-gram carb bread until after 11:00 A.M. And then I can't touch another pasta carb until 4:00 P.M. when I'm allowed two more carbs, but if I go power square dancing before four o'clock, I could increase the total carb intake to four grams."

Then came the *mishegas* these people on Atkins (and later the South Beach Diet) caused when eating in restaurants that did not prepare proper low-carb meals. How many times would we hear friends on the Atkins Diet tell a waiter, "We'd like the steaks done medium rare with nothing else. No potato of any kind. No pasta. Please take away the bread. And, if it's not too much trouble, please bring the steak on a paper napkin because if you set it on a plate, the plate might have served pasta or potatoes in the past month, which might leave a residue of carbohydrates."

It was enough to make you lose your appetite. And incidentally, the only person ever to die from the Atkins Diet was tubby Dr. Atkins.

SUICIDE BOMBERS
Dying is too good for you.

History is filled with suicide missions, some of them quite noble. Think of Samson bringing down the temple on the Philistines, or Davy Crockett and the brave Americans who stayed behind to defend the Alamo.

Perhaps the most famous example of sacrificing one's life for the so-called greater good were the kamikaze pilots of World War II. As the war was winding down in 1944, American forces were moving closer to Japan. Their pilots were outclassed, their planes were outnumbered and fuel was getting scarce, so the Japanese military devised a simple combat strategy: Create a suicide attack unit.

They loaded up planes with bombs, convinced some of their best remaining pilots to volunteer (though many believe they were forced), and began flying their planes into Allied carriers and battleships. Encouraged by some early successes, the Japanese even began building special aircraft for these one-way missions: planes with no landing gear.

By the end of the war, it is estimated, 4,000 kamikaze pilots were killed, but their efforts produced nearly 5,000 U.S. deaths, wounded an additional 5,000, and damaged scores of ships.

Today, of course, these same tactics are employed all over the world by suicide bombers. The difference, of course, is that instead of

killing soldiers in a war, these unforgivable attacks usually target innocent civilians—school buses with small children or commuter trains or
twin office towers filled with unsuspecting New Yorkers.

These current suicide bombers—or, as some call them, "Islami-
kazes"—claim that their missions are all in the name of Allah. (Never
mind that the Koran forbids suicide.) But what really motivates them,
we're sure, is that they're promised 40 virgins for becoming martyrs.

Call us crazy, but we bet there would be a lot less killing if they
asked to see them first with the veils off. We believe that after the veils came
off they would rather have had one live hooker than those 40 virgins.

NEARLY-
DEAD
SCHMUCKS

ARIZONA ROADRUNNER
Don't ruffle his feathers.

The United States has many species that are dangerously low in numbers and need to be saved. But sometimes the measures taken to preserve species do more harm than good.

For example, there's a tiny roadrunner in the Arizona desert that makes a strange chirping sound by batting its wings against the ground.

Ornithologists discovered that all types of human sounds disturb this bird. Today, the environmental laws prohibit anyone who lives within a 10-mile radius from waking up before 10:00 A.M. because the bird is a late sleeper and doesn't like to start its day until the sun is warmer.

Similarly, when local Arizonans are up, they can't walk too fast because tramping on the ground disturbs the bird and then it will throw a fit and refuse to breed—not unlike some of the girls we know. Also, these citizens cannot start cars before 11:30 in the morning because the bird would become nauseous.

Once there was a thriving factory in Arizona that employed a thousand workers. But it had to close because the smoke was giving the roadrunner a nasty case of sinusitis. The people were all thrown out of work, but at least the bird stopped sniffling.

Finally, it was decided to reroute traffic around the area inhabited by the bird. At first, highway engineers planned to go west but then discovered the new route would pass through the territory of a rare desert scorpion. Plans were changed to head east but, owing to all the other rare species endangered, the highway had to detour west to New Mexico and then circle back into Arizona. The cost was almost $700 million but at least no species was threatened with extinction.

This roadrunner is clearly in control. It doesn't matter that he has wings and can fly anywhere at any moment, he likes the Arizona desert and that's where he'll stay.

Unless of course he gets bird flu. In which case we'll kill the bastard.

CELEBRI-
SCHMUCKS

HARRY BELAFONTE
Tally him bananas.

Why do we hand crazy people microphones?

Harry Belafonte was once a respected activist. He protested with Martin Luther King Jr. in the 1950s, was blacklisted for his civil rights involvement in the 1960s, and helped finance Freedom Rides and organize the March on Washington in 1963. Impressive stuff.

But somewhere along the way all that steel drum music must have gotten to him. In the 1980s, he started defending the Soviet Union and Fidel Castro. And as soon as President George W. Bush got elected and invaded Iraq, the "Banana Boat Song" man went bananas.

In 2002, the King of Calypso criticized Colin Powell and Condoleezza Rice for serving in the Bush cabinet, saying, "There were two kinds of slaves. There was the house Negro and the field Negro. The house Negroes, they lived in the house with master, they dressed pretty good, they ate good 'cause they ate his food and what he left. . . . In those days he was called a 'house nigger.' And that's what we call him today, because we've still got some house niggers running around here."

Belafonte's hateful words were borrowed from Malcolm X, but Rice took the high road by responding, "I don't need Harry Belafonte to tell me what it means to be black."

Belafonte's craziest rhetoric, however, came just last year in

January 2006, when he called President Bush "the greatest terrorist in the world." He made these outrageous remarks not in the United States but in Venezuela, standing proudly beside the leader of that country, the notorious anti-American (and fellow nutcase) President Hugo Chavez.

When last we looked, President Bush risked his reputation and presidency fighting global terrorism, going after the bad guys in Afghanistan, capturing and bringing Saddam Hussein to trial, and trying to bring some nascent form of democracy to Iraq.

A few weeks later, Belafonte made some similar nasty remarks to an appreciative and mostly left-leaning crowd at the Arts Presenters Members Conference. To a standing ovation, he referred to the Department of Homeland Security as the new Gestapo.

Of course.

Whenever the mentally deficient run out of reason, the Nazi images begin to fly. And for what? Did Tom Ridge, the first director of Homeland Security, resemble Heinrich Himmler? Did Belafonte seriously think that because they make you take your flip-flops off at the airport or because the Feds may have listened to some heavy breathing on a few Americans' phones that we're living in 1942 Berlin? And let's not forget, this new security department exists because of an act passed by Congress and is subject to strict legal rules. The only rule the Gestapo followed was that they wore a lot of black leather.

Harry Belafonte may have been born in New York City, but he made his millions singing calypso ditties you can probably hear in any Jamaican marketplace. For free.

To him we say, "Daylight come. We want Harry go home."

KATIE COURIC
Anchor, away!

We used to love Katie Couric and believed she was great on the *Today* show, but honesty compels us to note the following: Perky goes a long way in this country, but one place it doesn't belong is behind the news desk. Walter Cronkite, Tom Brokaw, even Barbara Walters—these newscasters had and have gravitas. They deliver the news. They do not perch, one cheek on, the other off, the anchor desk. They do not crinkle their eyes or wear glittery lipstick. (Except maybe Chet Huntley.) They do not flirt with state officials. And they most definitely do not wear white after Labor Day as Couric did on her first CBS newscast.

Forgive us, but we don't want to hear about World War III from anyone named "Katie." A new strudel recipe, sure. But is it too much to ask that we keep the cute out of the news? Couric actually begins each broadcast with, "Hi, everyone!"—like she's hosting a potluck dinner.

Essentially she was brought on, and paid a whopping $15 million per year, to make the news friendlier. Why? That's what talk shows are for. Must everything be made nice for us? Does the news have to be reduced to pap? There are still a handful of grown-ups in this country. Men and women who want their information without entertainment. We *can* handle the truth. But we'd prefer to handle it from someone who spent less time on her hair.

Or showing off her legs. Back in 2003, Couric was a guest host of *The Tonight Show with Jay Leno*. Instead of using the regular desk that Leno sits behind every night, Katie Couric had the front of it cut away so that viewers could look at her shiny gams. Honestly, did Walter Cronkite even *have* legs?

Also, we'd like to not have to picture the inside of an anchor's colon. Now, we know that Couric's broadcast of her colonoscopy has led to record numbers of Americans getting tested and has probably saved hundreds of lives. But honestly, did you watch it? It's one thing for people on TV to have their heads up their own asses, but must the audience follow?

ROMAN POLANSKI
Thank heaven for English libel laws.

Publius Syrus, a first-century Roman writer of mimes, stated, "A good reputation is more valuable than money." But thanks to a lack of strong English libel laws, Roman Polanski, a 28-year fugitive from American justice, was awarded £50,000 (or nearly $90,000) in a libel verdict, to be paid by Condé Nast, the publisher of *Vanity Fair*. His suit claimed that the magazine stained his good name, which, considering he was a fugitive child rapist, was kind of like saying Dr. Josef Mengele had a poor bedside manner.

The libelous part of the article, written in 2002, was that Polanski attempted to seduce a beautiful Swedish woman on his way to the funeral of his wife, the murdered actress Sharon Tate. The incident allegedly occurred in Elaine's, the New York restaurant for the literati and glitterati.

In 1977, Polanski, the film director of *Rosemary's Baby* and *Chinatown,* had pleaded guilty to unlawful sexual intercourse with a 13-year-old girl. He was ordered imprisoned for a 90-day psychiatric study to help the judge decide the sentence. And then in 1978, Polanski fled to France where, presumably, rapists of 13-year-old girls are considered acceptable dinner guests. The reason for the flight to that lowlife nation was that he could not be extradited under that country's law.

Polanski gained unwarranted notoriety in 1969, when the Manson Family murdered his pregnant wife. The movie director has often used this terrible incident and also his imprisonment by the Nazis in a concentration camp to justify his unusual sexual proclivities.

In London, known in the legal trade as "Sue City," the normal burden of proof is different from that under the laws in the United States. Here, the defendant, the person being sued, has the burden of proof to demonstrate that the statement is true. In America, the person suing has the burden of proof to show that the statement is false. In the United Kingdom the defendant (i.e., *Vanity Fair*) had to illustrate that the story happened the way it was written. Additionally, in America, if the defendant is a public figure, for all intents and purposes, they are fair game, and rarely can sue for libel or defamation unless they can prove malicious intent.

The thrust of Polanski's claim was that the article made him appear "callously indifferent" to the murder and funeral of his wife. *Vanity Fair* asked in so many words that how could any vague statement—which it insisted was true and brought in witnesses to attest to the fact—that appeared in a magazine article damage the reputation of a fugitive from the law and sex pervert who had confessed to relations with a 13-year-old?

Sadly, the British jury found for Polanski—even though he had remained in France during the trial, phoning in his testimony. Literally. He argued that if he came to London, he faced extradition to the United States on the 28-year-old charge.

There are several morals to this tale. If you are a degenerate, planning to rape a child, it's prudent to learn to speak French. If you sue somebody for libel, all you need is a telephone and a smart English lawyer. And last, there is something in France that stinks worse than the people—and we believe it is the legal system.

MICHAEL RICHARDS
Little Bigot Man.

Trust us, being funny is tough work. Add to that the fact that comedians have as much right to be unfunny as anybody else—with occasional lapses of sanity and all-around offensiveness.

The fact is though that nobody wants to pay money to be insulted unless it's part of the act. To be offensive without offending requires surgical precision and separates a barroom bigot from a genius like Don Rickles. The former spews hate like water from an out-of-control fire hose. The latter focuses his comedic laser to uncover and then lacerate society's hidden hatred and pomposity. The audience's laughter, in turn, comes from the nervous self-recognition (or rationalization) that it's "the other guy" whom the comedian is talking about.

True hate, however, never engenders laughter—and audiences have infallible radar when it comes to detecting a comedian's intentions. That radar was clearly evident when Michael Richards—*Seinfeld*'s Kramer—performed at the Laugh Factory in West Hollywood last year.

There was nothing funny about repeatedly calling two men in the audience "niggers" or ranting that "fifty years ago we'd have you upside down with a fucking fork up your ass."

And just who is "we" anyway? As long as Richards wants to go back 50 years, maybe he should consider that a half century ago a Jew like him couldn't have gotten a job as a teller at any large bank. Or that he might have been run out of town by some nice fellas in white sheets. Astonishingly, shortly after the Laugh Factory episode, Richards was also accused of screaming, "you're a fucking Jew" at an audience member at a different comedy club in April 2006.

There is actually one bit of real humor in this otherwise ugly story. Days after the Richards story broke, California lawyer Gloria Allred appeared with two new clients: African Americans who were in the audience at the Laugh Factory that night asking for a retired judge to decide what the damages should be for listening to such hate speech. (Apparently, Allred believes that there should be a crime: boorishness in the first degree.)

And just what would those damages be? Keeping in mind that lawyers typically work on contingency in these types of cases (if we can even dignify this by calling it a case), Allred is probably looking at the return of the price of admission for the tickets. And that's not really the kind of money that will keep her bathing in Botox.

As for Richards, stick a fork in him. He's done.

SUSAN SARANDON
Is anyone Fonda her?

How much do we loathe Susan Sarandon? Let us count the ways. At the outset, let's acknowledge that, under proper direction, she gave fine film-acting performances in *Atlantic City* and *Thelma and Louise,* and an Oscar-winning performance in *Dead Man Walking.*

However, just because a person is absolutely first-class in one field does not mean she should be respected in another. A man may be a terrific delicatessen counterman but that does not mean that he can fly a plane to Milwaukee.

As an actress, Sarandon is first-class. As a political figure, she is no class. She also has a loud mouth, and is usually aiming it in the wrong direction for the wrong cause.

Any mother who named her firstborn son after a notorious, lower than lowlife scumbag murderer just to make some feeble and mistaken political statement is not our cup of mama loving. She had a child by her longtime companion, actor Tim Robbins. This son is named Jack Henry Robbins after Jack Henry Abbot, the infamous killer and onetime literary darling (*In the Belly of the Beast*) of the liberal intelligentsia. He was found hung in his prison cell at a New York correctional facility, the gruesome end of a murderous and murdering life. How would you like that for your namesake?

Since the hippy-dippy love-in years of the 1960s, other narcissistic Hollywood stars have tried to outdo one another in giving the most bizarre names to their children: Dweezil and Moon Unit Zappa, Ka-el Cage (that's Superman's name on his native planet of Krypton), and Sage Moonblood Stallone. We recall one B-movie couple who, in a hopeless stab at generating more publicity to advance their stagnated careers, named their dogs Mary and Phil, and their sons Rover and Spot.

But we digress.

Sarandon never met a demonstration she didn't like. Other couples with children invite parents of their kids' classmates over for coffee and cake. She invites them over for a march in the streets and hands out placards to mothers and children alike.

And if there is the possibility of being arrested before the cameras, so much the better. When there were demonstrations because of the tragic shooting of the illegal immigrant Amadou Diallo, celebrities like Sarandon showed up to be handcuffed by appointment. Sarandon, after a meeting with her hairdresser, makeup artist, and publicist, came to be arrested looking as happy as if she was going to a bar mitzvah.

The unworthy question crosses our minds: How is it that the Sarandons of the world never show up to be arrested in the middle of the night when there are no TV cameras around?

She is the prime example of why actors and actresses should speak only when someone else puts words in their mouths. Novelist John Le Carré once described an actress as a vessel waiting to be filled. Sarandon is a vessel waiting to be emptied. When she does speak for herself, it's all reheated and microwaved liberal gibberish.

Naturally, Sarandon and Robbins are charter members of many antiwar and anti–George W. Bush groups, most notably Not In Our Name (NION), an organization that pledges resistance to endless war. Outside of a lunatic asylum, who *would* be in favor of endless war? NION once issued a "Statement of Conscience" that denounced "unjust, immoral, illegitimate, and openly imperial policies towards the world," which is shorthand for global capitalism and the sentiment that whatever America does is wrong. The writer of this manifesto is "C. Clark Kissinger," a member of the Revolutionary Communist Party.

Politics has always made strange bedfellows but legitimate public expressions protesting the Iraq war not withstanding, the lesson that American history has taught again and again is *not* to find common cause with old Maoists or neocommunists as the liberal's alternative to unpopular domestic or foreign policy issues.

Sarandon has taken on the mantle of ex-activist/actress/millionaire Jane Fonda, whose self-absorption and egotism years ago during her well-publicized visit to North Vietnam bordered on treason. There she was dressed up in an enemy helmet, seemingly manning an antiaircraft gun, and applauding the North Vietnamese gun crew. Now Fonda explains that she happened by chance to be walking past the gun, and somebody offered her a hat and a seat, so she sat down. She didn't happen to notice that it was an enemy gun and that bombs were falling. In other words, today Fonda regrets the incident and promises the next time she will bring her own chair and wear an Easter bonnet with feathers to say no when the enemy offers another military helmet.

But Susan Sarandon continues with her condemnation of all things American, supporting Marxist and leftist movements for peace or for peasants around the world. Yet, she is still an active participant in the Hollywood star system, being paid a lot of money for her movie performances. Naturally, she has never advocated that the films she makes should become an economic communal sharing effort with everyone who worked on the big-budget pictures participating in the profits. But no matter.

If Sarandon feels so bad about all these poor people the United States is supposed to be hurting, why doesn't she contribute all the millions she makes in the movies? In fact, we will throw in a few bucks if it will shut her up.

STEVEN SPIELBERG
He lost it at the movies.

The film *Munich* depicts the assassination of 11 Israelis in the 1972 Summer Olympic Games. Anyone who witnessed that actual event on television has vivid memories of the hostage taking and the resultant massacre of the athletes by the Arab terrorist group Black September. And who can forget ABC announcer Jim McKay's simple but eloquent summation of this tragedy: "They're all gone."

In *Munich,* however, director Steven Spielberg added a second half to the story—the hunting of the terrorists and the retaliatory killing carried out by Israeli intelligence officers.

Clearly, this film should have been about the pursuit of justice: Bad guys commit heinous acts at the beginning, and virtue and righteousness prevail at the end. This was always the simple Hollywood formula before directors and producers were psychoanalyzed and decided they were learned pundits entitled to make political statements. Think of *Shane* or *High Noon*. There was no moral ambivalence in these westerns of the 1950s. Come to think of it, there was no ambivalence in *Jaws* either.

In creating *Munich, S*pielberg presented what he perceived was a balanced film but it angered us for two reasons: Basically the film suggests that Israel is to blame for existing at all, and the Arab murderers mouth self-serving justification for the killings on ethical grounds. Spielberg created a moral equivalency between the murderer and his victim, not content to concentrate on the spellbinding cat-and-mouse chase, he needed to explore the motivations of the Arab terrorists.

He knew the kind of movie he set out to make from the beginning, which is evident in his choice of the movie's coscreenwriter, *Angels in America* playwright Tony Kushner. Kushner is one of those liberal-progressive Jewish doves when it comes to Israel and Palestine. He is also a coeditor of *Wrestling with Zion,* a book that presents opinions from American Jews critical of Israel's right to exist, or overtly sympathetic to the Palestinians, or heaped with moral ambiguity about the conflict in the Middle East.

Admittedly, we shall never forget that Spielberg gave us the wonderful film *Schindler's List* and was also the generous founder of the Shoah Foundation, dedicated to remembering the survivors of the Holocaust.

But somewhere along the way, Spielberg volunteered to become part of that American Jewish ambiguity about Israel. He forgot who and what brought him to the dance and he made common cause with many of Israel's American and foreign enemies.

The result from this new, distressingly politically correct, approach is that the Oscar-winning director made a muddled, superfluous, and deeply insensitive movie called *Munich.*

Or, as it is known in German: *scheisse.*

BARBRA STREISAND
Mentl.

It turns out that people who need people are the *schmuckiest* people in the world. Okay, so obviously we're not big fans of Barbra Streisand's politics. She's stuck her famous nose out for lefty causes ever since she first sang "Happy Days Are Here Again" to JFK, and with the possible exception of Monica Lewinsky herself, Streisand was Bill Clinton's biggest champion for the eight years he was in office. (And speaking of lying in the White House, did it come as a surprise to anyone that the one night Streisand had her sleepover in the Lincoln Bedroom, Hillary just *happened* to be out of town?)

Since the 2000 election, however, Barbra Streisand has been one unhappy camper. For six years she's criticized the president for his policies in Iraq, global warming, and anything else that doesn't fit into her vision for America. In 2005, she even had the chutzpah to call for President Bush's impeachment because he took us to war "under false pretenses." Apparently, those so-called falsehoods didn't bother her too much when Clinton was prevaricating every time he opened his mouth. But then again, he was only guilty of perjury.

But even her cockamamy politics wouldn't bother us so much if she kept it out of her act. And we're not the only ones who feel that way. At a concert in New York in October 2005, one audience member got so fed up with the comedy routine she was doing with a Bush impersonator that he started heckling her. And how did Streisand react? She told this ticket buyer—a man who had paid hundreds to hear her sing—to "shut the fuck up."

Apparently she's no longer funny, nor a lady.

SCHMUCKS-IN-TRAINING

THE GAEDE TWINS
Neonatal Nazis.

In our most sordid nightmares, we never thought to consign two 13-year-old American girls to a list of lowlifes. But then a photograph of Lamb and Lynx Gaede showed the perky, adorable, blond twins from California wearing matching T-shirts with a drawing of the familiar yellow, smiley face. This happy countenance, though, sports Adolf Hitler's distinctly square black mustache and single swatch of black hair swept over the forehead.

The image of these innocent blond darlings looks like any other photo shoot found in teen magazines that advertise jeans, hair conditioner, sneakers, or acne cream, but the product the Gaede twins are selling is hate.

The twins are not attempting irony with the Hitler shirt. It's pure propaganda. When asked about the Nazi *führer,* Lamb told an interviewer, "Adolf Hitler was a great man who was only trying to preserve his own race in his own country." Lynx, not one to be left out of her sibling's odious slurs, chimed in, "I mean there were not even that many [six million] Jews alive back then. We knew there were concentration camps but they had swimming pools and tennis courts there."

Hate like this has run in the Gaede family for generations. April Gaede, the girls' proud mother, is the unapologetic member of Women for Aryan Unity, whose motto is "Securing our future one child at a time." The group's Web site is dedicated "to preserve the beauty, heritage and pride of our race." She is also the daughter of an avowed white supremacist named Bill Gaede. He professes passion for the swastika and its Nazi implications and has stuck the foul symbol on his belt buckle, pickup truck, and as the officially registered brand on his beef cattle. Apparently, his beef is the other white supremacist meat.

When the Gaede twins aren't posing in their not-so-Jewcy couture, they tour with their band, Prussian Blue. (The name refers to Zyklon B, the gas used in concentration camps. Holocaust deniers like the Gaedes claim that the absence of blue residue from the Zyklon B tablets proves that the extermination and genocide of millions never took place.) Prussian Blue songs are often dedicated to famous Nazi leaders like Rudolf Hess and their lyrics frequently drop Germanic touchstones (Vineland, Valhalla, and Fatherland). In a song entitled "Aryan Man Awake," the last lines exhort the faithful:

Who will face the end and watch a Valkyrie ride forth to
join the gods and fallen storm troopers of the north?

No doubt dedicated to the boys in the *bund*.

THE BIGGEST SCHMUCK OF ALL TIME

ROBIN HOOD
Ye Olde Schmucke.

That's right, the world's most beloved outlaw, Mr. Rob-from-the-rich-and-give-to-the-poor himself, is the biggest schmuck of all time. And here's why:

Robin Hood started out life, according to some historians, as the earl of Loxley, meaning this hero of the lower class was actually a nobleman who gave up his status to wear tights and hang out in the woods with his Merry Men. (We can't prove it, but we're guessing he would have been in favor of their being able to marry one another.)

And just who were these Merry Men anyway? Friar Tuck, Little John, Will Scarlet—not a Jew among them. (Although it's possible Tuck changed his name from Tuckerman to assimilate.) His choice of friends is significant because while Robin and his men were running wild in Sherwood Forest, the man they pledged their loyalty to was one of the great anti-Semites in history.

How big an anti-Semite was King Richard I? Let's put it this way, Mel Gibson should seriously think about making a movie about him. Richard actually forbade Jews from attending his coronation, and when some crashed his party anyway, he ordered them flogged. And those were the lucky ones. This in turn led to a hideous period in England where Jews were robbed, beaten, converted, and if that didn't work, killed.

Eventually, Richard left for the Crusades—again, not a good time for the Jews in the Holy Land—and allowed his younger, dimwitted brother John to seize control of England. Say what you want about King John, but he did sign a little thing called the Magna Carta. Meanwhile, Robin Hood and his men were stealing from the rich and giving to the poor.

In other words . . . they were Democrats.

AFFIRMATIVE ACTION

Nothing in our country is more insidious than affirmative action. Our goal is to have these laws voted out of existence. Affirmative action arose from the civil rights movement more than 30 years ago. We accept that many of these remedial laws and statutes ended years of minority discrimination against blacks, Hispanics, homosexuals, and women.

But today, when most of these problems have been resolved satisfactorily in the courts, it seems dumb to practice "reverse discrimination" by allocating special quotas and not pursuing the search for and the hiring of the best. This is the proverbial skim milk masquerading as cream, a pernicious quota system. And quotas—racial, religious, gender, political, etc.—are un-American, not to mention illogical.

Imagine that the U.S. men's and women's ski teams—predominantly comprised of athletes from New England, the upper Midwest, and Rocky Mountain states—were required to effect a more "balanced" team. Do we need a 350-pound Samoan-American sumo wrestler from southern California skiing the slalom?

The ski team analogy is no different from applications to law schools or medical schools that represent past battlegrounds for affirmative action cases that were decided by the Supreme Court. When you ask a doctor about her credentials, is it acceptable if she replies, "I graduated last in my class at college after nine years; however, because I'm an albino, bisexual, transvestite, Penobscot Indian with Tourette's syndrome, I was able to gain a place in med school. But don't worry, I must have left my scalpel somewhere in the OR, and, as soon as it's found, I'll start cutting."

You want to talk about affirmative action? Ask yourself this: Why are there no Jewish coal miners? Do you think that someone is preventing America's Jews from being coal miners? It's the same cultural reason; Jews don't go into mines with a light attached to their yarmulkes. Did you ever hear a Jewish man say, "I could have had a great career as a coal miner if the gentiles hadn't blocked my chances?"

Similarly, there are not a lot of Jewish hockey players. Is this a civil rights problem that can be corrected by affirmative action? Do you know of colleges whose priority has been to recruit Jews for the hockey teams? Let's face it; Jews have no interest in hockey. Simply stated, when sticks are flying around, Jews don't want to get involved.

We like to call the United States a meritocracy. So, until more Jews are playing hockey for the Rangers at Madison Square Garden, the country should shelve affirmative action.

AIR PURIFIERS

We know of a special hell occupied by the ghosts of useless products like hair growth formulas that do not work, crushed shells of crustaceans that claim to cure gout, and complex set-them-up-by-yourself exercise machines, whose only exercise provided is that of trying to put these metallic monsters together. Our nomination for this Useless Product Hall of Fame is the Ionic Breeze Air Purifier.

What if we invented a machine that costs $350 that rests in a corner, doesn't play music, doesn't connect to the Internet, doesn't show television, doesn't blow air around, doesn't cool or heat—but simply stands motionless without making a sound and sort of stares at you?

Would the American public be interested in such a product? You bet it would; Ionic Air Purifiers are selling off the shelves.

The machine advertises that it is equipped with "Ozone Guard." We always thought ozone was good for us and one of the environmentalists' major complaints has been the widening of the hole in the ozone layer. The ever-increasing hole allows bad stuff into the earth's atmosphere that may cause foot fungus and perhaps cancer. So, why is the Ionic Purifier claiming it keeps the ozone out if ozone is healthy for us?

In California, at least two lawsuits have been filed seeking class-action status for consumers who bought the Ionic Breeze Air Purifiers from Sharper Image. And in November 2004, the U.S. District Court for the Northern District of California dismissed a lawsuit that Sharper Image brought against the magazine *Consumer Reports* over its assessment that the Ionic Breeze Air Purifier was "ineffective" as a cleaner, and produced "almost no measurable reduction in airborne particles."

Take our advice, don't buy the machine, and save money. Instead, buy a copy of *Consumer Reports* for a few dollars and fan yourself.

AIRPORT SECURITY

The distinctly delicious Chuckles jelly candy colors are red (cherry), yellow (lemon), black (licorice), green (lime), and orange (three guesses). Oddly enough, this is not dissimilar from the red, orange, yellow, blue, and green colors of the terrorist threat level system. Were these gelatinous candies the model for the five-color terrorist warnings? More important, did the color-coding succeed in making us safer or did it increase the consumption of Chuckles?

And what about some of these other so-called safety measures at the airport? Like the preposterous questions asked at the check-in counter and their expected but never-given answers:

> AIRLINE ATTENDANT: Did you pack your own
>   luggage?
> PASSENGER: My friends, a three-person terrorist cell from
>   Al Qaeda packed it.
> AIRLINE ATTENDANT: Did anybody else handle your
>   luggage?
> PASSENGER: Yes, my same fanatical terrorist pals.
> AIRLINE ATTENDANT: Has your luggage been with you
>   the entire time?

PASSENGER: No, first it traveled to a bomb-making factory
and then it was returned to me at the hotel.

AIRLINE ATTENDANT: Thank you. Have a nice
flight.

Only a security expert with the brain of a cashew would
think that a terrorist would answer these ridiculous questions truthfully.

As for that other kind of screening, we do not believe in racial or
ethnic profiling, considering that this discriminates against people un-
justly and also violates tenets of American democracy. But still, we pon-
der, why, when passing through the nation's airline security gates, do we
never see stopped for questioning any 20-year-old Muslim men in caftans
and white crocheted wool skullcaps, carrying the Koran, burning in effigy
little dolls of Uncle Sam, and instead, we always see 80-year-old Jewish
grandparents who have been pulled over and strip-searched for carrying
nail clipping tweezers? The truth is the new screening machines are basically tweezer detectors.

Since 9/11, the Department of Homeland Security has uncovered close to three million tweezers, about 90 percent seized on the New
York to Miami or Fort Lauderdale and return flights. Every one of these
tweezers was attached to a key ring carried by an elderly Jewish person.
What this means to us is that unless terrorist weapons are attached to key
rings, these will never be discovered at the airport.

It did not help that, when all these new security measures
were put into place, President Bush encouraged the nation to be alert
but not be nervous, to keep an eye out at all time for suspicious activity but to go about our business in a normal fashion. Nor were we
buoyed by Secretary of Defense Rumsfeld's suggestion that Americans
actively hunt down possible terrorists roaming free in the country. Did
Rumsfeld anticipate that seniors in old-age homes were going to put in

their dentures and hunt down the world's most dangerous terrorist and say, "The game's up, Osama buddy; you're coming with us"?

All of these new security measures bring to mind a T-shirt we saw for sale on the street in Manhattan. It depicts five tough-looking Native Americans in full war dress standing under the slogan: "Homeland Security since 1492."

AUTOMATIC TOILETS AND SINKS

A frustrating experience is trying to wash your hands in an auto-mated system in a men's room. (It may also exist in women's bathrooms but unfortunately our investigations were inhibited in this regard. We don't mind wearing a simple strand of pearls, perhaps, even a touch of rouge in a flattering shade, but to go into a women's bathroom for investigative purposes would have required a major operation and on some book research we drew the line.)

The automated sink system was designed for efficiency but it is not easy to use.

Inside, you place your hands under the sink to start the water because it's computerized—the sink not your hands. But the hands have to be in the precise spot for the electronic beam to start the flow of water. If they are one centimeter to the left or to the right, or your hands are Munchkin-sized, nothing happens.

Well, eventually, something *does* happen: terrible aggravation and your blood pressure shoots up and jumps off the charts. Now, you have become the schmuck that stands at the sink for minutes moving your hands around, hoping that by chance they will land on the magic spot that hits the beam that starts the water that begins the process of washing and that allows you to exit the bathroom with clean hands and get on with your life.

Self-starting sinks may be annoying and frustrating but they are not as exasperating as automatic toilets. It's bad enough to spend 30 minutes waving your hands under the faucet hoping for a drop or two of water but inside the toilet all you require is a quick flush and a hasty exit. This will not be the case.

The toilet system operates under the same concept as the sink; it's supposed to *know* when to flush automatically. You're a considerate kind of person so you wait inside the stall for the anticipated *whoosh*. But nothing happens. So, you move your ass to the left and then to the right, hoping that these random movements will start the flushing process. Meanwhile, with shifting your rear end to the left and to the right you start to resemble a dancer in a rumba contest at Roseland.

Nothing happens. And there's no handle to push or pull. No button to press. No voice-activated command. And you are trapped by your own delicate sensibilities.

Exasperation begins to come over you in waves and heightens when a burly voice outside the stall questions, "Hey, you done in there?" But no matter how many different ways you try, the toilet refuses to flush and you've become a prisoner of the stall.

You want to do a friend a favor when he enters an automated toilet? Send in a sandwich and a book.

DOCTORS WHO KEEP YOU WAITING

When did doctors decide our time was worthless? Your time means nothing to them. If you're late or cancel you pay anyway. After hours of waiting, the doctor (who looks as though he just finished playing nine holes) will explain the wait as "It was an emergency." We think that people who are made to wait should charge the doctor *their* hourly rate.

KIM JONG IL

This is what happens to a person when you start wearing Joseph Stalin's old hair. It seems that every twenty minutes North Korean leader Kim Jong Il is threatening to blow up some part of the world with nuclear weapons he may or may not have, or showing off his goose-stepping army. (Can they actually fight or are they just auditioning for the Rockettes?)

But just how seriously can you take a threat from a man who reportedly loves James Bond movies, *Friday the 13th*, and *Rambo*, and watches a lot of NBA games? Is it possible this world potentate is actually just a teenage boy?

INSURANCE COMPANIES

You buy a policy and spend a fortune. Then, when it's time to collect, the company pays you, reluctantly, and then follows up with a 30 percent raise for the following year's premium. The next time, you're afraid to report the theft (accident) because of the fear of higher rates. So you self-insure the lower-costing damage and will wait to make a claim only for a catastrophe. But the real catastrophe is the catastrophic annual premium. And, once having made a claim, you're placed on the company's list as a troublemaker and complainer. The only people being insured are the insurance companies. Our premiums provide the monies to keep them insured.

The most egregious example was insurance companies not paying flood insurance after Hurricane Katrina because, they claimed, the wind drove the water into the houses. It was wind damage for which no one had taken out this type of insurance. We ask rhetorically, "What happens to insurance companies when their offices are flooded?"

THE IRAQ PANEL

magine for a second that you were a chef and wanted some advice on creating a new marinara sauce. Would you call the best plumber in your city? How about the smartest lawyer? Or maybe the best five doctors? Of course not. If you want to know how to make the best tomato sauce, you'd call up a bunch of other chefs and ask their opinion.

So why was it that this bipartisan diplomatic dream team anointed to solve the situation in Iraq didn't include a single general? James Baker, Sandra Day O'Connor, Vernon Jordan, and the other brainiacs who issued their meaningless report last year may be brilliant in their respective fields—although in Jordan's case that field appears to be helping his friend Bill Clinton get Monica Lewinsky out of town by obtaining a job for her in New York—but they were never going to solve Iraq's problems for one simple reason: None of them are generals.

They might as well have asked Mario Batali what to do.

PAUL MCCARTNEY

This is one of those cases that keeps Raoul up at night: You're worth more than a billion dollars and you marry a gold-digging model, but because she loves you (yeah, yeah, yeah) you don't want to have a prenup.

Heather: You mistreated me, abused me, made me crawl around on one leg to wait on you.

Paul: You're lying. I never did any of those things.

Heather: I have proof—a tape recording. It's all on the tape.

Paul: Oh, you have proof? Why didn't you say so in the first place?

Well guess what, schmuck, she may have lost a leg, but this divorce is about to cost you that plus an arm.

BILL MAHER

We believe Bill Maher is a generally funny and talented guy. And for obvious reasons we are willing to forgive a few obnoxious, tasteless, and occasionally clueless comments from comedians. You can't expect every joke to kill. Or even wound. Just ask that old Borscht Belter John Kerry, who, something tells us, won't be asked to play the big room at Caesars any time soon.

One of Maher's comedic lowpoints came a few years ago when he decided he owned the English language, particularly the phrase "Politically Incorrect" and sued us. Of course this ridiculous lawsuit was thrown out by a federal judge.

We don't hold that against him anymore, but we *were* angry when he got out his pom-poms to cheer on the 9/11 assassins in 2002 saying that, "staying in the airplane when it hit the building, say what you want about it, it's not cowardly."

Not cowardly? To our thinking it does not take a brave man to slit a helpless flight attendant's throat and use an airplane to assassinate thousands of defenseless people whose only crime was going about their daily business.

But Maher didn't stop there. He also questioned the bravery of our armed forces whom he cited as ". . . cowards, lobbying cruise missiles from 2,000 miles away."

After the understandable outrage, trembling on the brink of career suicide, he apologized a few days later for his "punch lines." But a careful reading of his formal apology omitted the terrorists and limited his contrite words to our armed forces.

The American people are generous and forgiving, they have taken Maher back (at least in TV terms), but he should do the right thing now and apologize properly. Don't be a coward.

PSYCHIATRISTS WHO DISAPPEAR IN AUGUST

If you live in any large city, you can't go crazy in August. If your wife hits you with a meat cleaver on August 5, you won't be able to visit the therapist until after Labor Day. If it's a Jewish therapist, you can't book an appointment until after the Jewish holidays at the end of September. Anyone who puts up with this kind of service should have his head examined.

PUSHY WAITERS

You know the type. They introduce themselves and then narrate their life story, complete with Social Security number and their mother's maiden name. Then, for the next hour and a half, they offer to grind fresh pepper on everything you ordered. Is the pepper on the table not fresh enough? If not, maybe you should think about not putting it on our table in the first place. Also, if the dish needs fresh pepper so badly, maybe the chef should have cooked it better. Then, while you're still eating, they come by and remove plates before you've finished. And finally, you hand over a $50 bill for a $6 tab, and they ask without looking at the check, "Do you need change from this?"

BRITNEY SPEARS

We know what you're saying—why Britney Spears and not her soon-to-be schmuck of an ex-husband? Here's why: Because he married a multimillionaire pop star and will walk away from the marriage set for life. While she will be left raising his idiot children and financing his stripper habit. Look, anyone can make a mistake when it comes to marriage, but this was her *second* one—and she's, what, 14?

How bad is her taste in husbands? Let's just say Elizabeth Taylor sent her a thank-you note.

SUDDENLY JEWISH POLITICIANS

Years ago there was a famous skit on *Saturday Night Live* featuring Tom Hanks as the host of a game show called "Jew, Not a Jew?" The parody presented the names of famous Americans and the game show's contestants guessed whether the people were Chosen People.

In recent years, much to our amazement, it seems that either discovering or claiming Jewish ancestry has been a potential boost to a public career. In the past, politicians running for national office would have shied away from announcing a heritage that traced back to the learned Rebbe Glassburg in the shtetl of Viznitz or to the Jewish all-female klezmer musicians of Lodz. Years ago, they stated that not only were they not Jewish, but they had never seen a Jew, or thought they had ever seen a Jew, heard of a Jew, or spoken to a Jew.

But today, politicians have an army of genealogists looking for some trace of real or possible Jewish ancestry. To this we simply say, *Oy vey!*

Secretary of State Madeleine Albright was the first person to be surprised by the revelation that she was a Jewess with deep and old cultural roots going back to Prague's Jewish community. Her reaction, "It is a duality I will have to live with for the rest of my life." Well, "duality" is not the same as "distinction." "Duality" means Dr. Jekyll and Mr. Hyde and hardly suggests any pride; it is more like a social disease she didn't know about, but is resigned to live with.

Second to board the "I'm a Jew" bandwagon was, oddly, Hillary Clinton. This startling revelation came at about the same time as this Arkansas resident, originally from Illinois, decided to run for senator from New York, a state with a large Jewish population.

The heretofore Methodist Hillary Clinton connected the dots back to a supposed Jewish ancestry via a questionable route. It seems that Hillary's mother's second husband was Jewish!—a fact that the senator had forgotten over the preceding years. Remember, traditionally the only way to verify whether or not a child was Jewish, was to ascertain that she was born of a Jewish mother. Although Mrs. Clinton's mother never converted to Judaism, and all of this Jewishness occurred after the fact of Hillary's birth anyway, using Hillary Clinton's "geometric logic," had our widowed mothers remarried a down-at-the-heels Romanov, we could claim our candidacy as the future co-czars for the throne of Russia.

Meanwhile, during George H. W. Bush's presidency it came out that Secretary of Defense James Baker had uttered the phrase "Fuck the Jews." Naturally, the popularity of the Bush administration plummeted; its leaders were condemned as horrible anti-Semites. But, later, when it was reported that Mrs. Clinton made similar vulgar remarks, calling someone a "fucking Jew bastard," these same Jews did not believe her accuser even after he passed a lie detector test.

Our favorite newly minted Jew, however, is Senator John Kerry, the 2004 Democratic nominee for president. He was outed by his hometown paper, the *Boston Globe,* when it revealed that his grandparents were originally Kohns from Austria who had converted to Roman Catholicism in 1896.

Kerry replied, "This is amazing. This is fascinating to me." What proved more intriguing was that to find another, more gentile sounding name, grandpa Otto Kohn dropped a pencil on a map of Europe. It landed on Kerry in Ireland. Had the pencil rolled a centimeter to the west, it would have hit on the quaint Irish peninsula town of Dingle.

We look forward to seeing Senator Dingle and the rest of his new political *meshpucha* at our next seder.

TOURISTS

A distinct difference between American gentiles and American Jews is how each group goes away on vacation.

For a gentile, a vacation is as simple and easy as packing the tent and tying the bicycle on top of the car. The family heads to the nearest state park, where it unpacks several loaves of white bread, huge jars of peanut butter and jelly, and instant lemonade mix. For exercise everyone takes nature walks through the forest and plays with a Frisbee. Cost for the week's vacation? Maybe $100.

A Jewish family is only interested in a faraway destination that involves airport limousine service and plane travel that was purchased as a terrific deal that this family could find and you could not.

Then there is the question of the gym. When calling for reservations, an old Jew makes sure the hotel has the latest state-of-the-art gym. The likelihood of his using the equipment is about the same as his taking an overdose of prune juice. But when the man returns home he will boast, "We had a gym fit for King Kong to do exercises."

And why fly first-class? Why not? A person will pay 10 times as much for a wider seat. If your rear end is not larger than normal, you will never use the extra five inches of seat. But rich people are embarrassed to be seen flying coach because it offers no status. If you spot a well-known, wealthy person sitting in coach, he'll answer that he's sitting in that section waiting for someone to exit the bathroom.

Also, first-class passengers love to hear the announcement in the terminal, "We're now loading first-class passengers only." And then we all look to see who are the people that could pay 10 times as much. Naturally, the yentas say, "That woman doesn't look like she could afford to fly first-class." The men say, "My secretary must have made a mistake. I only travel first-class."

Now consider the Grand Canyon. Visiting this natural wonder is emblematic of the difference between gentiles and Jews. To gentiles, the Grand Canyon is a marvelous, natural site and they are always so anxious to see it, they shout to the family, "Hurry up, come see the *crevasse*."

What's the hurry? says the Jew. It's really just a huge hole not going anywhere. It was there hundreds of millions of years ago and it's not moving away. When a Jew sees a wide-open hole in the ground, it's a chance to sue somebody.

EPILOGUE

After we finished writing this book, while celebrating over a glass of vintage celery tonic, our editors crashed the festivities by asking us to add one more section describing why each of us believed the other to be a schmuck. From our pedestals of absolute perfection we were, naturally, offended by this request and immediately demanded our money back. Whereupon, our editors uncharitably reminded us that they gave *us* the money, and, if we did not do as requested, they would ask us for *their* money back.

And let's face it, unless we are part of an army, Jews are not particularly tough.

So . . .

Why Jackie Mason Is a Schmuck
BY RAOUL FELDER

Like Tom Cruise, Mel Gibson is another movie star who seems to have left the Earth's orbit in the last few years. (At least Cruise has the excuse that his religion believes in aliens.) As for Gibson, he was always one of the most beloved actors until his career started being driven by his fundamentalist Catholic views. Or, more to the point, by his anti-Semitism.

In 2004, Gibson cowrote, directed, and produced *The Passion of the Christ*, a movie about the last 12 hours of Jesus's life. Gibson financed the movie himself because no studio wanted to put up money for a film that was made in Hebrew, Aramaic, and Latin. Even before the film was released, Gibson was accused of making an anti-Semitic movie. It didn't help that he claimed in an interview that the Holy Spirit was "directing the film through him."

And when *New York Times* columnist Frank Rich (and you know how we feel about him) wrote that *The Passion of the Christ* would incite anti-Semitism, Mad Mel responded by saying, "I want to kill him. I want his intestines on a stick. I want to kill his dog."

It also didn't help Gibson that his father has long been known as a Holocaust denier. But does Gibson repudiate his father's hateful beliefs? Of course not. In 2004, he told an interviewer, "The thing with him [my father] was that he was talking about numbers. I mean when the war was over they said it was 12 million. Then it was six. Now it's four. I mean it's that kind of numbers game."

Of course, the most damning evidence that Gibson is anti-Semitic occurred in July 2006, when Gibson was pulled over by the police on suspicion of drunk driving. You know the rest. He started swearing and abusing the arresting officers, shouting, "fucking Jews . . . Jews are responsible for all the wars in the world." He then asked one of them, "Are you a Jew?" In fact, Sheriff's Deputy James Mee was. (Gibson's ranting didn't just include anti-Semitic views, though. This Hollywood sex symbol, long loved by women, also made a hideously sexist comment when he turned to one of the female officers and said, "What do you think you're looking at, sugar tits?")

What made the whole episode so distasteful was what happened next. Gibson admitted he was drunk, claimed to have a severe alcohol problem, and asked for forgiveness. And was even granted some.

Abraham Foxman, the longtime director of the Anti-Defamation

League, turned the other cheek after Gibson's transparent mea culpa, saying: "This is the apology we had sought and requested. We are glad that Mel Gibson has finally owned up to the fact that he made anti-Semitic remarks, and his apology sounds sincere. We welcome his efforts to repair the damage he has caused, to reach out to the Jewish community, and to seek help." Or perhaps Mel sobered up and remembered that a couple of executives in Hollywood might be Jewish. A few moviegoers as well.

Even more disappointing than Abe Foxman's defense of Gibson was another prominent Jew who rushed to Gibson's side. This clueless entertainer claimed that Gibson has always been "a mecca of decency all of his life," and has "never offended a Jew in his life personally."

Mel's unlikely ally didn't stop there. "How a guy lived for 50 years is what should count, not one remark when you're drunk! He never joined a club that was anti-Semitic; he never refused to give a guy a tip at a restaurant because he found out he was Jewish. His house doesn't have a sign in front of it that says 'No Jews Allowed.' What did he ever do that's anti-Jewish in his life? A whole 50 years of decency doesn't count because he made one remark? Now they say, 'apologize!' But he didn't apologize enough; he should apologize a little higher. He should apologize in the morning; he only apologized at night. He should apologize at least two more times, four more times, 32 times. They won't be happy until he gets circumcised!"

What schmuck said all of this, you ask?

Jackie Mason.

Why Raoul Felder Is a Schmuck
BY JACKIE MASON

It will come as no surprise, but I buy my suits wholesale, sometimes even at cost. Anybody who doesn't do this is a schmuck. In fact, I have a friend who buys his suits *below cost*. (I know, I know, I can already hear you asking, "Below cost? How can a garmento make any money selling suits below cost?" Simple. He sells a lot of them.)

But not Raoul. Everything Raoul owns has to match, and for the privilege of having his socks match his underwear, Raoul spends his clients' fortunes.

Look at a self-conscious Jew who walks into a fancy restaurant. Everything matches. The shoes match the belt, the cuff links match the jacket, the watch matches the fancy pen in his pocket, even the soup stain on the tie matches that disgusting pattern on his pocket square. Now look at a gentile who goes into the same restaurant. Blind people dress better. But why should gentiles be concerned with how they dress? They own the country. I try to explain this to Raoul, but he is too stubborn to admit that dressing well is his own sickness.

Me, if one leg of my trousers was shorter than the other, it would not bother me. I'd just buy a house on the side of a hill.

Below cost.

BRAND SCHMUCKING NEW

AFTERWORD

A pparently some people don't like to be called schmucks.

We thought we had written a book—hopefully funny to some, irreverent, thought-provoking, argumentative—but still a book. We were wrong. It turns out *Schmucks!* was an explosive device—a sort of literary IED—that caused a crisis in the judicial process in the state of New York.

On April 17, 2007, the *New York Post* ran a headline—"Raoul Defiant"—with the subhead "Refuses Gov's Demand to Quit," and beneath that, two photographs: one of Raoul and the other of the recently elected governor of the state of New York, Eliot Spitzer. Neither photograph would have suggested a beauty contest winner. One might wonder about the genesis of all of this *mishegas,* and since Raoul was the one maligned, we'll let him tell you . . .

New York, like other states, has a regulatory body that entertains complaints about judges: the New York State Commission on Judicial Conduct. I am its chairman, having been elected unanimously by the members of the commission. The commission members themselves are selected by leaders of the various branches of government, some by the governor of

New York, some by the chief judge of the state, and some by the various legislative leaders. Needless to say, some members are considered political hacks appointed by other political hacks.

Now, it should probably be noted at this point that there is a fundamental distinction between a judge and a member of the commission. Judges are paid a salary and, in return for taking the king's shilling, they receive a pension, health benefits, and have to accept many restrictions on their outside activities, while commission members (with the exception of several who are judges) are private citizens. We receive no money, no pension, no health care, and we donate our time periodically. (I know, I know, who's the schmuck?) Oh wait, the chairman also has his name on a plaque that one sees on the way to the men's room.

Prior to my being elected chairman, Jackie and I had written several books together, many op-ed pieces, and countless articles, so the members of the commission knew precisely whom were electing.

Dr. Freud said he didn't believe in coincidences. Maybe he was right. But in this case, there were three events that all happened about the same time: First, there was a family court judge, Marian Shelton, who was under investigation by my commission. The proceedings of the commission are secret, but Judge Shelton, spending in excess of $100,000, took out *two* bizarre full-page ads in the *New York Times* acknowledging publicly that she was under investigation and also denouncing me, the commission, and, in one of the ads, the president of the court officers union.

The second event was the Don Imus "nappy-headed hos" incident, which set the stage for a sudden rash of sensitivity.

And the third event was the publication of this gentle book in March 2007.

While there is no direct proof of this, I believe that Judge Shelton, perhaps because she was under investigation, sent a copy or copies of the book weeks after its publication to members of the new governor's administration. Soon afterward, in a routine telephone discussion on the business of the Commission on Judicial Conduct with the new governor's counsel, David Nocenti, he suddenly turned the conversation to what he considered to be offensive parts of our book. Nocenti mentioned to me two offending passages (obviously, these had been previously marked off for him). One was a section on Saudi Arabia, which begins as follows:

> Other than the togas worn in the days of the Holy Roman Empire (which was hardly holy or Roman, and which, eventually, no longer even qualified as an empire) we never cared much for men who wear bedsheets as clothing. Like the Ku Klux Klan. And the Saudis. . . . The Saudis control 25 percent of the world's oil reserves and this has allowed them to blackmail us. For decades, successive American Presidents have acted as if Saudi oil was more important than Israeli blood.

The above is not exactly a startling comment—at least, it should not be, to any American. In fact, less than a month later, an article on the front page of the April 29 edition of the *New York Times*—hardly a conservative publication—indicated that Saudi Arabia "effectively torpedoed" American efforts to work out a resolution of the Palestinian problem, and quoted the Saudis' characterization of America's presence in Iraq as "an illegal foreign occupation."

Mr. Nocenti also quoted to me part of another passage in the book, one about the Reverend Al Sharpton: "We actually kind of admire Al Sharpton, the longest, unsustained, unsponsored carnival in America." This statement is rather mild when it comes to Sharpton, but you could see where the politicians were going. The mice were about to scatter.

During the conversation, I tried to point out several things to Mr. Nocenti, mainly that there is still a First Amendment in America, that this is a humor book, and that there is even a cartoon on the cover picturing Jackie and me in superhero costumes. I kept saying, "These are jokes; don't you get it?"

Apparently he didn't.

Then the snit hit the fan. People began to be driven by their own ambition, insecurities, pretentiousness, fear, and, most of all, hypocrisy. On Friday, April 13, late in the afternoon, the commission issued a vote of no confidence in me. This, too, would have died a quiet death because all votes are made in private, except that the commission put out a press release, saying that *Schmucks!* repeatedly employs racial, ethnic, and religious invective. They must have assumed that by their flogging me with the word "racial" I would be fatally wounded.

Hardly.

In point of fact, they obviously didn't read the book (although in the hope that the commission would actually read it before passing judgment, I sent a copy to each member, nicely inscribed). There is no racial invective in here. Indeed, Fredric Dicker of the *New York Post*, who obviously *did* read *Schmucks!,* confirmed in an April 16 *Post* article that "there were no explicit examples of racial insults and several statements in favor of racial equality."

There are, however, a few "ethnic" pieces, but the commission neglected to mention that these four essays involved folks who are (more or less) enemies of the United States. There are pieces on "Humorless Muslims" (the people who wanted to chop the hands off a Danish cartoonist), "Suicide Bombers" and Yasser Arafat (under "Dead Schmucks"), and on Iran's charming president Mahmoud Ahmadinejad.

Should we apologize for making jokes at their expense? These aren't exactly people you'd want to invite to your next seder.

The commission made two further points. They first criticized me for a tongue-in-cheek use of the word "allegedly" in a piece about Benon Sevan, who is now avoiding extradition in Cypress for embezzlement. It seems they neglected to read to the end of the piece, where we underscore the fact that this has not been proven by saying things like "If bribery can be proved" and "If Sevan is convicted."

Then they pointed to the first sentence in a piece on affirmative action, "Nothing in our country is more insidious than affirmative action," taking it quite literally. Now, really! How many of us have said, "This is the worst meal I ever had." Does that mean the speaker never had, in his entire life, a worse meal? "You are the most beautiful girl in the world," etc.

The commission neglected to mention that in the first paragraph of this very same piece Jackie and I acknowledge that "remedial laws and statutes ended years of minority discrimination against blacks, Hispanics, homosexuals, and women." We then go on to point out that it would not be welcome to a man on the operating table if the doctor said to him, "I graduated last in my class at college after nine years; however, because I'm an albino, bisexual, transvestite, Penobscot Indian with Tourette's syndrome, I was able to gain a place in med school."

The bottom line is, many Americans are in favor of affirmative action today and many are not. (Incidentally, subsequent to the publication of the book, Barack Obama indicated that he also believed that the concept of affirmative action should be phased out.)

In a series of press conferences, Governor Spitzer first indicated that he was going to begin a lawsuit, then toned down his approach, suggesting we should see how this "plays out." Since then I have repeatedly invited the commission or the state to begin a lawsuit to have the matter tested in the courts. To date, those opposed to me have been disinclined to test it. There is still a First Amendment alive and well and living in America—as the courts would so find.

The last public comment on this matter appeared in the popular Page Six column of the *New York Post*.

STILL STANDING

RAOUL FELDER is still definitely serving as chairman of the State Commission on Judicial Conduct, despite the efforts of his fellow commissioners to oust him last month. The mostly liberal panel members cited what they deemed to be inappropriate humor in "Schmucks," the book Felder co-wrote with Jackie Mason. They expected the divorce lawyer to step down meekly, but he decided to fight instead. Now his foes seem ready to quit. "I've heard of people giving up after a battle and during a battle, but I've never heard of people giving up before a battle," Felder told Page Six. "Not even Sanjaya did that."

I have often been asked, "Why didn't you simply go along and resign the chairmanship?" The answer is one that's self-evident to anybody of my background: I did it for the next person who doesn't have as big a mouth, or the energy and means to fight back. So Jackie and I will keep speaking our minds, keep making jokes. And you should, too.

On to some new schmucks. . . .

THE SPITZER ADMINISTRATION
What didn't they know?
And when didn't they know it?

Not long after the *Schmucks!* contretemps described in the afterword, New York governor Eliot Spitzer, Mr. Clean himself, was accused of employing some dirty political tricks.

We think highly of Mr. Spitzer. He enjoyed our best wishes for a successful term in office and we view his present predicament with more sadness than *schadenfreude*.

The facts, as they came out, suggested more than a mere scandal and, in fact, possible potential criminal liability. Indeed, at the end of the road it could result in the impeachment of the governor—which would be an awful thing, coming mere months after an overwhelming electoral victory.

The story is a simple one. Apparently New York State government resources were utilized by the governor, or those around him, to discredit a political opponent. After that, a Watergate-like flurry of activities was uncovered—basically a cover-up. Key people involved would not cooperate with the investigation of the New York State Attorney General's Office. The Attorney General's Office did not have subpoena power, and members of the governor's staff, relying on this, would not testify under oath. Rather, they submitted a self-created, selective, carefully worded affidavit. There is now even a further question concerning e-mails that were hidden. In all, one aide was suspended for a month and another was transferred. Hardly serious penalties.

Polls show that at least 50 percent of the people polled in New York State did not believe Governor Spitzer. For the governor's version to be believed, there would have had to exist in his brand-new administration a conspiracy by his aides about which the governor knew nothing. The governor should be given the benefit of the doubt, but as virtually all observers have noted, it is hard to accept the fact that the governor—particularly this governor, who micromanages things—was totally unaware of what had occurred, as well as the subsequent attempt to cover it up.

One character in this drama has so far gotten a pass: David Nocenti, the governor's counsel. His name appeared once in the *New York Times,* but, other than that, the media have basically glossed over him. It should be noted that he was the one instructing Governor Spitzer's staff to refuse to testify under oath and, in fact, recommended that these staff members be appointed special counsel so they could invoke the attorney-client privilege. If they had nothing to hide, why would they need to invoke such protection? (Technically, the privilege belongs to the client, *not* the lawyer. And in this case, the governor is the client. Therefore, the question becomes why would he want to hide behind a wall of silence?)

Now, in life things do not often come around full circle, but perhaps in this case they do. It was Mr. Nocenti, we believe, who was responsible for the no-confidence vote directed at Raoul by the New York State Commission on Judicial Conduct and all the surrounding hoopla we discuss in the afterword. Again, we'll let Raoul tell you:

Mr. Nocenti, in my dealings with him, was arrogant and also, perhaps, a bit not too smart. While I will not reveal the conversations I had concerning the commission, one colloquy stands out:

I made the commonsense suggestion to Mr. Nocenti that the governor, at least once, come meet with all the members of the commission, have a chat with them, shake their hands, and maybe give a bit of a pep talk to the staff. Nocenti immediately turned this down. I then suggested that the commission could go to *his* office for a meet-and-greet session, enabling the members to feel that the governor took an interest in the activities of the commission. One would think the governor would be interested in this, all the more so because the state of the judiciary was one of the areas he had laid title to in his bid for election (although he was not an advocate for an increase in their budget, which eventually happened because of the perseverance of the legislature). Despite this, Mr. Nocenti's answer to me was "The governor already knows you and [another member], and, as to the others, so what?" It seems obvious that he said this without consulting with the governor.

It is hardly a comforting thought that any senior public official should have such an attitude toward a state conduct commission or that he should be advising the governor.

We deserve better than a government run by schmucks advised by schmucks.

ALEC BALDWIN
Mr. Pig Mouth.

We're no fans of Alec Baldwin's politics and, frankly, between that and his cockamamie activist statements over the years, we could have included him in the hardcover version of this book.

Baldwin once referred to President Bush as a "trust fund puppet." He has called Dick Cheney a "terrorist" and a "Constitution-hating sociopath." And he once described our friend Sean Hannity as a "no-talent whore."

Basically, this guy puts the jerk in "knee-jerk liberal."

But in April 2007, Baldwin was caught saying something so despicable that even he finally had to apologize. You know the story: Baldwin and his ex-wife, Kim Basinger, were involved in an ugly divorce, which led to an even uglier legal case over custody of their daughter, Ireland. When his daughter didn't get on the phone for a scheduled call, he left a disgusting message on her answering machine in which he called her a "rude, thoughtless pig."

And that was one of the nicer things he said.

Oh, and did we mention she was 11?

Now listen, Raoul knows a thing or two about nasty divorces. And it's rarely one person's fault. Even a loudmouth like Alec Baldwin would not have lost his temper like that unless he'd been seriously pushed to the brink by his ex. But there is simply no excuse for talking to a child like that.

And he knew it.

A few days after the tape of his rant was released to the world, Baldwin issued a sincere public apology to his daughter and announced that he was writing a book.

On parenting.

SENATOR LARRY CRAIG
John Juan.

As far as we're concerned, what a man does in the toilet is his business. But when Idaho senator Larry Craig was arrested for lewd conduct in a Minneapolis airport men's room in June 2007, he made his business ours.

According to the police report, the Idaho senator sat in a stall for several minutes and tapped his right foot toward the man in the stall next to his, which was evidently a signal that the would-be Gene Kelly wanted to engage in homosexual activity. Either that, or he has a catchy tune in his head.

What happened after that became a classic case of he said–he said—the arresting officer and the senator dispute the facts—but what is not open for argument is that nearly two months after his arrest, Senator Craig pleaded guilty to disorderly conduct.

When news of his guilty plea hit the newswires, it soon became clear that because of his men's room episode, Senator Craig had flushed his political career down the toilet.

Which is where the ensuing debate remained as well.

He might be gay. He could be gay. He's not gay but he used to sing in a barbershop quartet.

Again, we're not interested in what a man (or a woman) does in private. What troubles us in the Larry Craig story is that a senator pleaded guilty to behavior unbecoming to an elected official. And in doing so, he paid his fine and signed the papers, which included the clauses "I understand that the court will not accept a plea of guilty from anyone who claims to be innocent" and "I now make no claim that I am innocent of the charge to which I am entering a plea of guilty."

Not long after the story broke, Senator Craig did what we believed was the right thing: he agreed to step down as senator. And then he changed his mind and vowed to fight the charges against him.

At this point, we don't care what happened in that men's room but we do know this—this story stinks.

O.J. SIMPSON
Stop, you're killing us.

Did you really think O.J. Simpson was just going to go away? Or, like us, did you assume he would be so busy looking for the real murderers of his ex-wife and Ronald Goldman on the golf courses of America that he wouldn't have time to make headlines again?

First came his disgusting book, *If I Did It,* in which he outlined how he would have committed the double murders he has always claimed he didn't commit. We thought the only person who would read this heinous book would be Phil Spector, but amazingly it rose to number 2 on the *New York Times* bestsellers list, just ahead of a new book by the other great liar of our time, Bill Clinton.

Then, just as *If I Did It* was getting ready to be released, Simpson was back in the news again for being part of a conspiracy to steal some memorabilia (which he claims was stolen from him) at gunpoint in a Las Vegas hotel suite. Simpson was arrested a few days later and charged with, among other things, kidnapping, robbery, and use of a deadly weapon.

Frankly, we don't have the stomach to endure a *third* O.J. trial. We just want him to go away. Say, for 30 or 40 years.

DON IMUS
Ho no!

Honestly, was anyone actually surprised by the Don Imus story? Think about it for a second. For nearly 40 years, Imus has been given a few hours a day to say whatever he wants on the radio. The man's a shock jock, for God's sake—an occupation he practically invented. (Okay, so it's not exactly like discovering the polio vaccine, but it's something.) You think he's not going to offend some people with his humor now and then? Please, he's paid millions to offend people every day.

So what made calling the women's basketball team from Rutgers "nappy-headed hos" so explosive? Simple—he picked on the wrong people.

You want to make fun of Bill Clinton? Or Ted Kennedy? Or anyone else who's rich and famous and powerful? Have at it. You can even wear tiny boots, a half-gallon hat, and pretend you're a cowboy while you're doing it.

But what did these girls do to deserve getting kicked by Imus's spurs? They played basketball. And they played it well, representing themselves and their school with tremendous class.

To Imus's credit, he offered what seemed like a sincere apology, both publicly and privately. He even went on Al Sharpton's ridiculous radio show to say he was sorry. Why anyone should have to apologize to

Sharpton is a mystery to us. Asking Al Sharpton for forgiveness after making a senseless racist joke is like apologizing to O.J. Simpson for being mean to your wife.

Still, the damage was done. Don Imus had to be punished, despite his numerous apologies and despite all of the extraordinary charity work he has done over the years.

But like any comedian, he got the last laugh. A few months after he was fired, Imus successfully sued CBS for breach of contract and is now back on the air. And making more millions.

Proof that there's no business like ho business.

ROBERT NOVAK
Plame Thrower.

In every generation there arises a radical new anti-Semite who uses the pulpit of the popular media to explain (in the most dramatic and seductive terms) how the current world crisis can be explained in just three words: "It's the Jews." The Jew-hating bigot of the moment is unquestionably Robert Novak.

Novak disdainfully calls the situation in Iraq "Sharon's war"—implying that a military action that has cost thousands of American lives (and jeopardized countless more) was really just for Israel's sake. How is it that no one else has, or claims to have ever had, any evidence of such a hidden, nefarious motive? And that Mr. Novak himself offers none?

Meanwhile, Novak plays the old "American Jewish lobby" card—implying that alleged Jewish power, influence, and financial status amount to a controlling machine—before which politicians and the military cower in fear and shrink back from daring to criticize Israel's purported wrongdoings. Mr. Novak is quite right that there is a lobby (AIPAC) for Israel, as there are lobbies for everything—smoking, drinking, bed-wetting, you name it. But he vilifies the Israeli lobby at every turn. Why? Because he is an anti-Semite.

Why does Novak think that there is a murky, conspiracy behind the United States's support for Israel? Can't the reason be simply that

America recognizes the "rightness" of Israel's cause, that Israel is the victim and not the perpetrator of all the killings in the Middle East? Of course not.

Then again, what kind of moral compass can you expect from a man who famously outed CIA operative Valerie Plame and then acted as if he had done nothing wrong? Basically, Novak is the kind of man who starts the bar brawl with a cheap shot to your chin, then offers to hold your coat while you fight with the rest of the schlubs.

But to date, there has been nothing more heinous than Novak's studiously pretentious moral outrage to any Lebanese casualties suffered in the conflict between Hamas and Israel. After all, where was Mr. Novak's "compassionate" human spirit—not to mention his journalistic sense of outrage—while Israelis were regularly being injured, maimed, and killed for decades in cafés and restaurants, supermarkets, stores, hotels, and on her streets? Or is it perhaps Mr. Novak's beliefs that only Arab lives are worthwhile and only their injury and loss are to be lamented?

By far, Novak's most egregious claim concerning the Lebanese war is that Israel was saved from a public relations nightmare following its attack on Qana by the distraction of Mel Gibson's anti-Semitic, drunken tirade. Only a desperate, distorted hater could see the tragedy of Qana as the fault of the Israelis. How many lives are the Israelis obligated to lose before they acquire the moral right to attack the arsenals of destruction used against their population? Trust us, Mel Gibson isn't nearly as dangerous as Bob Novak. After all, Gibson only has a messiah complex, whereas Novak takes pride in being called the Prince of Darkness.

In light of the above, it might surprise you to learn that this same anti-Semite was actually raised Jewish and converted to Catholicism in 1996.

They can have him.

ANNA NICOLE SMITH
Who's your *meshuggeh* daddy?

We have a simple philosophy: we don't speak ill of the dead, with the hope that they return the favor. But in the case of Anna Nicole Smith we can't remain silent.

She ran what could charitably be called her love life like a bakery: pick a number and stand in line. Unfortunately, we never made a trip to that bakery, so we are part of a very small group of men who can definitively claim they are *not* the father of her daughter, Danielynn.

Apparently, Anna Nicole was egalitarian with her charms, an equal opportunity provider. Age, religion, nationality, and ethnicity played no role in her romantic choices—and for this we applaud her (particularly for the age part).

Prince Frederic von Anhalt—who allegedly purchased his title on eBay and who once sued Pfizer, the maker of Viagra, because, he said, it made him impotent—was one of these characters who lined up to be the father of Anna's child. (If it had turned out he was the father, he should be *paying* Pfizer, rather than *suing* them.) When the reporters asked him how his 90-year-old wife, Zsa Zsa Gabor, would react to his announcement, he replied that she was free to sue him for divorce. He neglected to point out that at the age of 90, most people can hardly make the trip to the toilet, let alone to a lawyer's office.

Another contestant in her Baby Daddy Sweepstakes was the minister of immigration in the Bahamas. He also allegedly slept with Anna Nicole, presumably in an effort to speed up her effort to immigrate to the Bahamas. We must uncharitably observe that sleeping with him might be a good reason for somebody to speed up their emigration *from* the Bahamas.

The driving force behind this final *meshuggeh* farce in her brief but epic *meshuggeh* life was, of course, money.

Her existing will, which named her attorney (and putative lover) Howard K. Stern—this schmuck warrants his own entry and gets one, next—as her executor, trustee, and guardian, has flaws large enough for Anna Nicole at her blimpiest to float through.

For instance, California does not, except under certain circumstances, allow a caregiver to inherit under a will. And Stern, arguably, fits into this category. (After all, leeches were once used medicinally.) Once this issue is considered, as far as the will is concerned, there is the not insignificant question of her mental capacity and any possible duress.

But should all of that mess sort itself out, paternity, particularly when the will is set aside, carries with it serious financial rewards. Just being executor of the estate, at a commission rate of two and a half percent, may bring in over a million dollars in fees. Not to mention the guardian-parent's lifestyle under the guise of support for the child.

Come to think of it, maybe, we *should* have gotten on that bakery line.

HOWARD K. STERN
The K is for Klassy.

What a piece of work this guy is. Chutzpah doesn't even begin to cover it. Howard K. Stern first came to prominence as Anna Nicole Smith's attorney in her infamous inheritance case following the death of her 2,000-year-old husband, J. Howard Marshall. He later became a punch line (and a punching bag) as Smith's Man-child Friday on her car accident of a reality show. Watching her slur abuse at him each week apparently put the fun in dysfunctional for some people.

But then their story got truly ugly.

Barely two weeks after the tragic death of Anna Nicole's son in September 2006, Stern "married" Smith and proceeded to sell their wedding photos for $1 million.

Not even five months after that, Smith herself was dead and Stern, claiming that he was the father of her daughter, Dannielynn, refused to take a paternity test to prove it. (A DNA test finally showed that one of Smith's ex-boyfriends, Larry Birkhead, was in fact the father of her child.)

Subsequent allegations about Stern and Birkhead are so crazy that it makes us long for the good old days when Anna Nicole was just an incoherent golddigging stripper.

But when it comes to gold digging, it turns out she had nothing on Howard K. Stern.

FUNDAMENTALIST ATHEISTS

In God they mistrust.

People have been picking on God since, well, God only knows. We don't worry so much about the Lord in these situations— we think he can take care of himself. Our problem is with this new breed of atheist who feels the need to belittle people of faith. Any faith.

In his bestselling book *The God Delusion,* Richard Dawkins lays out the case for why God doesn't exist: essentially, the universe is so vast and complex that it is inconceivable that one supreme being could understand it all, let alone create it. He goes on to point out that every genius throughout history—Thomas Jefferson, Albert Einstein— questioned the notion of a supreme being. In other words, he's saying to the reader: Look Einstein, only a schmuck like you would still believe in God.

There are others in this atheist choir—writers like Christopher Hitchens and Sam Harris, who page after page remind us of all the hideous acts that have been done throughout the ages by every major religion. And it's true. A lot of awful things have been done in the name of God.

So have a great many good things.

As far as we're concerned, we don't care if you're Jewish, Christian, Muslim, atheist, or agnostic. Just don't let your faith get in the way of anyone else's.

And if it turns out that there is no God and there is no heaven, the fundamentalist atheists of the world can have the last laugh.

But if the Richard Dawkinses of the world are wrong?

God help them.

DAVID HASSELHOFF
On second thought, let's hassle the Hoff.

David Hasselhoff became famous for two things: talking to a car and wearing a Speedo. For the latter, we suppose, a small debt of gratitude is owed. After all, were it not for *Baywatch,* we would not have enjoyed all those scenes of women in bathing suits running in slow motion to rescue some poor drowning schmuck.

As for *Knight Rider,* the series in which Hasselhoff first became famous, let's just say it made *Baywatch* look like *Hamlet.* Our problem with it wasn't that Hasselhoff talked to his car—Jackie once had an uncle who sang to his toaster—it's that the car talked *back.* And today, whenever you get in a car with a fancy shmancy navigation system, you have to listen to it tell you to make a right turn in two blocks. Or that you left your lights on. Frankly, we thought cars already came with a system for telling you that you missed a turn—it's called wives.

Of late though, Hasselhoff is renowned for episodes in which he seems to enjoy his schnapps a bit too much. There was the time he was asked to leave the matches at Wimbledon (he denied he had been drinking), the time he was escorted off a plane for being unfit to travel (again, he denied drinking), and the time he was so drunk that one of his daughters actually videotaped him shirtless eating a hamburger off the floor.

Even Ronald McDonald finds this clown embarrassing.

ALEX RODRIGUEZ
Yankee panky.

We're Brooklyn guys. You know this. So it will come as no surprise that we don't exactly root for the Yankees. But even lifelong Yankee fans have a hard time cheering for Alex Rodriguez.

It's not because he makes more money per at bat than your average public school teacher earns in a year. It's not even because he likes to sunbathe shirtless in Central Park or that he looks like he wears blue lipstick (or maybe he's just cold all the time?).

No, the reason that baseball fans (even ones who wear pinstripes) think A-Rod is an A-hole is that he plays with no class. Never mind that he could easily end up hitting more home runs in his career than Barry Bonds and that he will surely be enshrined in Cooperstown. Being an all-time great has never been an excuse for bush-league play—like the time in the 2004 American League Championship Series that he tried to swat the ball out of the pitcher's glove to avoid being tagged out at first. Or the game in 2007 when he was running to third and yelled "Mine!" to distract a third baseman from catching a routine fly (he dropped the ball). That's the kind of stuff that a Little League coach would bench you for.

But when it comes to cheating, apparently Rodriguez doesn't limit himself to the baseball diamond. In May 2007, the *New York Post* ran a story (with photos) about A-Rod having dinner with a blonde

D-cup. A D-cup who was not his wife. The two later went to a strip club and then headed back to his hotel in Toronto. For late-night mah-jongg no doubt.

Oddly enough, Mrs. Rodriguez didn't appreciate this story too much. A few weeks after it ran, she was photographed during a game at Yankee Stadium, wearing a T-shirt with words that rhyme with "Pluck You."

Something tells us she'll be calling Raoul's office very soon.

ROSIE O'DONNELL
Preaching from the bullying pulpit.

For many years, Rosie O'Donnell made a career out of being the Queen of Nice. No problem—plenty of comedians adopt a persona as part of their shtick: Jack Benny was cheap. Rodney Dangerfield couldn't get respect. And Rosie was nice. (Jackie, by the way, just pretends to be a Jewish tummler. He is actually a shiksa housewife from Connecticut.)

Then one day, Rosie decided she didn't want to be so nice anymore. She started speaking her mind on issues like gun control, presidential politics, and 9/11. Even her comedy act got mean.

By the time she landed as the moderator on *The View*, there was no stopping Rosie and her cockamamie opinions. One week she was shooting her mouth off about Catholicism, the next she was attacking Donald Trump. It's hard to say which of these rants is the most offensive, but for us two stand out: Rosie claimed that 7 World Trade Center was actually imploded on purpose—by whom she wasn't sure—to cover up financial scandals at Enron and WorldCom.

A few months after that, Rosie said of American troops in Iraq, "655,000 Iraqi civilians dead. Who are the terrorists?" Eight days later, Rosie was off *The View*, thus ending our friend Barbara Walters's long national nightmare. But make no mistake, we haven't heard the last of the new Queen of the Obscene.

IMMIGRATION OPPONENTS
We're not on the fence about a fence . . .

We have a simple solution to the immigration debate. But first, why do we talk about the immigration *problem?* We have an immigration problem when people fight to get out of a country, not to get *into* one. What we have here is something between "a condition" (like when your mother-in-law has bursitis) and a "situation" (like when a lowlife neighbor keeps parking in your driveway).

Here, free of charge, is our three-part immigration solution:

1. *Registration:* The most powerful weapon police have is "intelligence" (and we mean that in the military sense). When a cop stops you for a traffic violation, in two minutes he or she can find out if you are wanted for anything from spitting on the sidewalk to murder. Similarly, if a crime has been committed in a neighborhood, the police can immediately do a computer search and obtain records of other similar crimes in the neighborhood, helping them to identify suspects.

What we need to do is much the same: develop a comprehensive central registry of all aliens—legal and illegal—in America. An immigrant not having the proper identification card should be deported immediately and should never be permitted to reenter the country.

Eventually all of the illegals will either be sent to jail or, over the course of time, die.

2. *Fences:* The idea that we cannot build a suitable fence or have secure borders is ridiculous. We have had secure borders in Germany, North and South Korea, Vietnam, etc. The 1,500-mile-long Great Wall of China was built in the third century BC and still looks pretty formidable.

In this regard, we have an additional simple solution: Just give anybody who will live on a U.S. border two free acres of land. Thousands of people will happily live there and keep an eye on things, pick up the phone if they see anybody coming from Mexico, and offer them coffee and cake until the border patrol arrives. Of course, the Miami Beach condominium market may decline, but we think it's a fair trade-off.

3. *Draft Boards:* For those immigrants who register but are *not* here legally, we should establish local community boards, similar to the local draft boards we had during World War II. These boards would be made up of small groups of dedicated citizens who would hear cases involving illegals. In that way, local community standards, which usually vary, would be applied. Only after this process is completed would the aliens be permitted to appeal adverse decisions through the judicial system.

What we don't want to be, of course, is a country that denies health care to a child or adult, denies education or any other benefits that, on a human level, a functioning humane democracy should provide. Without immigrants, we would have no atomic age, no computers, no lasers, no microchips (thank you, Mssrs. Einstein, Teller, Fermi, et al.).

Too often the people who want to crack down on immigrants are like members of a country club who, once admitted, don't want to let anybody else join (not unlike those rich schmucks in *Caddyshack II*). It should be suggested to them that without immigrants we would not even have an America.

LINDSAY LOHAN
Fully loaded.

When we were young, our mothers used to tell us to be sure to go out with clean underwear on just in case we were hit by a bus. Why this made sense, we couldn't tell you. It seems to us if you actually *did* get hit by a bus, underwear would be the least of your problems. But we wore clean underwear anyway.

Clearly this lesson has been lost on young women in Hollywood today. Britney Spears, Paris Hilton, and now Lindsay Lohan have all been photographed—more than once, it should be noted—showing off what we can only presume they think is their best side.

If going commando was the only trouble Lohan got herself into these past couple of years, we could forgive it. (Don't get us wrong. It's not that we don't want to see you without your underwear. It's just that we'd rather see you this way in private.) But it seems that every week she's photographed drunk or getting into another car accident or drunk after getting into another car accident. You'd think with her kind of money someone might suggest a chauffeur?

What makes her story all the more sad is that somewhere along the way, Lindsay Lohan clearly had talent. She could act, she could sing, and she was easy on the eyes.

About the best thing we can say about this sad girl now is that she isn't Britney Spears.

Yet.

MICHAEL MOORE
Icko.

It's a good thing Michael Moore walks around with a camera. Otherwise he'd just be considered a stalker. After all, Moore has built a career out of ambushing people—some famous, some not—and making them look foolish on film.

Of course, tricking people like that is nothing new. But when, say, Allen Funt played his pranks on *Candid Camera*, he did things like have people hide in mailboxes to make his victims laugh. Moore's games are far more dangerous. Far more cruel.

For nearly 20 years, in gimmicky movies like *Roger & Me, Bowling for Columbine,* and *Fahrenheit 9/11,* Moore has sucker punched his subjects with his left-of-Karl-Marx politics and his when-did-you-stop-beating-your-wife–style questions. Whether he's blaming automotive executives for economic woes in his hometown of Flint, Michigan, or damning the NRA for senseless violence in a Colorado high school, Moore only knows how to shower blame. He doesn't bother to offer solutions to the impossible problems he exposes. After all, it's much easier to make the downtrodden (or powerful) look stupid.

Frankly, we thought Moore couldn't get much lower than when he interviewed Charlton Heston—then the head of the NRA and the man who played Moses himself—about gun control in *Bowling for Columbine*. Now, if you want to pick on Moses that's your business. (But just remember what happened to the last guy who tried that.) And it wasn't enough for Moore to make fun of Heston's well-known and sincere passion for the Second Amendment. No, he had to try to make Heston look like a racist, too. The only problem with that—Heston is someone who marched with Martin Luther King Jr. (And this was long before every star in Hollywood figured out it was a good career move to embrace liberal causes.) Trust us, the world would be a much better place with more so-called racists like Charlton Heston.

What made Moore's assault on Heston so hateful, though, was that this beloved actor was suffering from the early stages of Alzheimer's. The only defense for behavior like that we can imagine is that Moore needs his victims to be mentally impaired to have a fair fight.

Did we mention that Michael Moore received an Academy Award for this dreck?

It got worse after that. Moore's next movie, *Fahrenheit 9/11,* set out to make President Bush look like a buffoon in his handling of September 11. The film contained so many lies, distortions, half-truths, and other manipulative techniques that it should have been named an honorary Clinton.

And then came *Sicko,* a movie that tried to make a mockery of the American health care system. And how did Michael Moore do this? By showing how two longtime thorns in our country's side—France and Cuba—do everything better, cheaper, and with more compassion than we do.

To which we say, if you really feel like America's such a horrible place, Michael Moore, if you really think they have a better life in Paris or Havana, then *au revoir. Adiós.*

Get the schmuck out of here.